ALEXANDRE
DUMAS

Introduction
"Black French Author"
and translation by
Dorothy Trench-Bonett

Charles VII
at the Homes of his
Great Vassals

The Noble Press, Inc.
Chicago

Library of Congress Cataloging-in-Publication Data:

Dumas, Alexander, 1802–1870.
    [Charles VII chez ses grands vassaux. English]
    Charles VII at the homes of his great vassals : a tragedy in five
acts / Alexandre Dumas, père : introduction and translation, Dorothy
Trench-Bonett.
        p. cm.
    Translation of: Charles VII chez ses grands vassaux.
    Includes bibliographical references.
    ISBN 1-879360-00-4 (pbk.) : $10.95
    1. France—History—Charles VII, 1422–1461—Drama. 2. Charles VII, King
of France, 1403–1461—Drama. 3. Africans—France—History—Drama. I. Title.
II. Title: Charles 7th at the homes of his great vassals.
PQ2225.C3E54   1991
842'.7—dc20   90-63426
                                                                    CIP

Translated from 1831 edition, Charles Lemesle, Paris.

Noble Press books are available in bulk at discount prices.
Single copies are available prepaid direct from the Publisher:

Marketing Director
The Noble Press, Inc.
213 W. Institute Place, Suite 508
Chicago, IL 60610

To my father, my mother, and my husband—
for love, support, and encouragement;
and to Michael, Jr., and David—
for patience.

CONTENTS

INTRODUCTION

I. *The Dumas Family: Three Generations of Blacks in France*

ALEXANDRE DUMAS *père* (1802-70) was the grandson of a French nobleman—and of an African slave. Not much is known about Marie-Cessette Dumas, his grandmother, who would bequeath to three generations of famous Frenchman both her color and her family name. She died in 1772 in Haiti, which was the French colony then known as Sainte Domingue.[1] It is not known whether she was born on that West Indian island or in Africa (although the fact that she had a French surname probably means that she was creole), nor is it known from which African people her ancestors came. Many Haitians have their roots in Dahomey — *vaudun*, the religion still practiced there, was originally the Fon people's religion.[2] But Haiti, like the rest of the West Indies and the United States, took in blacks from all of the West African nations, and Marie-Cessette Dumas could have been descended from any of these. It is not known how she caught the eye of the young man calling himself Antoine Delisle, who had come to Haiti to make his fortune in the 1730s—a young man who was really Antoine-Alexandre, the future Marquis de la Pailleterie.[3] It was recorded, though, that he paid "an exorbitant price" for her, probably because she was, by European standards, a beauty.[4] Once this price was paid, of course, she had no choice about becoming his lover; she was his property. They lived together for more than twenty years, until she died. She bore him four children: Adolphe, Jeannette, Marie-Rose and Thomas-Alexandre.

In 1772, when Antoine–Alexandre decided to return to France to reclaim his estate in Normandy, he left three of his children behind. Like their mother, they were legally his property, and he arranged a fictitious sale of them to a friend "on whom he could rely to treat them well." Perhaps they still have descendants living in Haiti. Thomas–Alexandre, the youngest child, born in 1762, was the Marquis' favorite; he wanted to bring him back with him to his own country. So the nobleman brought his black son to Port–au–Prince, where he "sold him to a ship's captain in return for his own passage." But he asked the captain to keep the boy with him and "put him on a ship to France as soon as his father [the marquis] had sent the necessary money."[5] And so Thomas–Alexandre, the future General Dumas, arrived in Europe in 1776, listed in the records as the "slave Alexandre," property of a Lieutenant Roussel. He went to live with his father in the suburb of St. Germain–en–Laye, outside of Paris.[6]

So far, this is not an unusual story. The Marquis de la Pailleterie was not the first European who decided to go to the New World and rebuild his family fortunes with black slave labor. Nor was he the first white man to take a black concubine. This practice was widespread throughout the Americas. In the southern part of our country, public opinion was against it, and mulattoes were generally not acknowledged by their fathers, but this was not the case in other parts of the New World. In Brazil, the British West Indies, and the Spanish, Dutch and Portuguese American colonies, it was not uncommon for white men to acknowledge black children, free them, educate them and leave them property. Many Frenchmen brought their mixed sons (though not their daughters) back to France. There were so many *gens de couleur* (blacks with some European ancestry) in France on the eve of the French Revolution that the Chevalier de St. Georges, a black French nobleman, was able to form a regiment composed completely of men of color.[7] But, although free mixed black people had privileges in the French colonies and were often wealthy, prejudice against them was extreme. If they could, they preferred to live in France. They faced prejudice there, too, as we shall see, but it was not comparable to the situation in the islands, where a free man of color was "excluded from the naval and military departments, from the practice of law, medicine and divinity, and all public offices or places of trust," and could have his right arm cut off if he ever struck a white man.[8] "Colored" was a term used to mean anyone with African ancestry—even if the person had one African great-great-great-great-great-grandparent and 127 who were white.

Obviously, Thomas–Alexandre could compare life at the court of Louis XVI and Marie–Antoinette to what his position would have been back in Sainte Domingue and know he was privileged. Not only was he free, but he was the acknowledged heir to a marquisate. The Davy de la Pailleterie family dated back to the sixteenth century,[9] had registered proof of its nobility in 1710 and 1712, and owned a castle in Normandy, at Bielleville–en–Caux.[10] However, it seems that the handsome young man, who was a very dark–skinned mulatto (portraits of him show that he did not look mixed but resembled a pure–blooded black), was made to remember, often, that he was not really considered the equal of a white man. On one occasion, while at the theatre with a white female friend, the young black was insulted by a Frenchman, who first tried to get the woman to come away with him. He called Thomas–Alexandre a "lackey" and a "half–breed" when he objected, saying that if they were in the West Indies, the black "would be fettered hand and foot."[11] When Dumas *père* told this story in his memoirs, he said that his father took revenge for these insults,[12] but what actually seems to have happened is that the woman left the theatre and "Thomas–Alexandre returned to his box, trembling with rage."[13] I don't know whether the author revised the story himself or was told an incorrect version by his father, but Thomas–Alexandre probably wished that he could have "thrown his insulter bodily out of the stalls and subsequently wounded him in duel," as the story Dumas tells recounts.[14] Thomas–Alexandre got some satisfaction though, as the other whites who were with the rude Frenchman forced him to apologize to the black man.

Other things besides his race concerned Thomas–Alexandre. He was continually at odds with his father, the Marquis, who in his old age had turned out to be a miser. Thomas–Alexandre, "trained to no particular profession, with no friends to help him to a career, depended entirely on his father's good will."[15] It was an intolerable situation. When the Marquis married his housekeeper to save money, Thomas–Alexandre, whose position as heir was now in jeopardy, joined the army. The father flew into a rage because the son had enlisted as a simple soldier, and forbade him to use his aristocratic name when serving so low in the ranks. So Thomas–Alexandre took his mother's name, Dumas. The Marquis died a short time later, in 1786, but Thomas–Alexandre renounced the title as well as the Davy de la Pailleterie coat of arms, taking as his slogan *Deus dedit, Deus dabit*, meaning, "God gave, God will give."[16]

God *did* give. When the French Revolution began three years later in 1789, Thomas–Alexandre left the Queen's service (the regiment he had originally joined was the Queen's dragoons) and joined the Revolutionary Army. Most French blacks took the same side. Who had more reason than they did to long for changes? Who believed more than they did in liberty, equality, fraternity, and the rights of man? For a while it seemed as though some of the changes that they hoped for would take place: white revolutionaries, such as the Marquis de Lafayette and Robespierre, agreed that it was sheer hypocrisy to talk of equality and fraternity while black slavery continued in colonies that were the property of France. "You urge without ceasing the Rights of Man, but you believe in them so little . . . that you have sanctified slavery constitutionally," Robespierre charged during the debates about abolition in the Assemblée Nationale. "Perish the colonies if the price is to be your happiness, your glory, your liberty!"[17] Slavery was not abolished, and Robespierre's government soon fell; he was so willing to let those who did not agree with him perish that he was largely responsible for the Reign of Terror. But the times were much more liberal than they had been under the Old Regime, and this was good for blacks.

In former days, under the old system of patronage and privilege, Thomas–Alexandre would have remained in the low ranks of the army forever, but now he was treated as his abilities deserved, and he "had a remarkably swift series of promotions. In July 1793, he was named *général de brigade*; barely two months later, *général en chef* [commander-in-chief] of the army of the Western Pyrenées; three months after that, *général en chef* of the army of the Alps, fielded by the government of the Revolutionary Committee of Public Safety. The next year he was made commander of the Brest Coast, and then *général de division* on the Sambre–et–Meuse. Later he commanded all calvary in the Italian campaign, then was appointed head of a calvary division at Mantua."[18]

Not only was Dumas quickly promoted, but he also quickly became famous for the remarkable feats he performed, feats that would seem incredible if so many witnesses had not vouched for them. The most famous of these exploits was probably his single-handed defense of the Bridge of Brixen, at Clausen in Austria, against an entire enemy squadron. "As the bridge was narrow, only two or three men could confront him at a time and Dumas sabered everyone who approached him. He was wounded three times and his coat was pierced by seven balls, but he stopped the enemy charge."[19] The terrified Austrians nicknamed him "the black devil." The color of his skin was also remarked on during the French invasion of Egypt: "his brown color . . . resembling the Arabs, strongly impressed the garrison." Napoleon, who was in charge of the armies by then, noticing this, "sent for the mulatto general and ordered him to head the garrison vanguard intruding inland, so its members could see the skin of the very first general they had to deal with was not of an unfamiliar hue."[20]

The black general soon fell out with Napoleon, though. It had become obvious that Napoleon's ambitions did not match the ideal of a republic. Dumas was brave enough to tell his colleague that he did not approve of these ambitions. Thus, though the black man's exploits were just as extraordinary in Egypt as they had been elsewhere (his prowess in battle caused the Arabs to call him "the angel," after the exterminating angel of the Koran),[21] Napoleon soon was beginning to hint that Dumas was stupid. "Intelligence is not his strong point," the Corsican is supposed to have said to the senior medical officer of the French army about Dumas.[22] He began to refer to the general not by his name but as "the colored man."[23] When Dumas, on his way back to France from Egypt, was shipwrecked off Naples and imprisoned by the anti-republican Bourbon government, Napoleon made no move to try to free him. It may be relevant to recall here that it was Napoleon who, by trickery, captured another black man who believed in equality, the great Haitian general Toussaint l'Ouverture, and let him die in prison in 1803.[24]

Thomas–Alexandre did not die in prison, even though he was poisoned there.[25] In 1801 he was allowed to return to France — crippled, half–paralyzed, tormented by ulcers — a broken man. He returned to his family in the small town of Villers–Cotterets, where in 1792 he had married a French girl. Her name was Marie–Louise, her maiden name was Labouret, and the couple already had an eight–year old daughter. Soon after they were married, the couple had another daughter, Aimée. On July 14, 1802, another child was born to them. Named after his father and grandfather, he was called Alexandre Dumas.

The new baby lived, at first, in luxurious surroundings. The Dumas household was renting a little castle, called Les Fosses and had a cook, a gardener, and a *garde*; the general had a valet, Hippolyte, who was, like himself, black.[26] These prosperous times, however, did not last long. The general's health had continued to fail ever since his imprisonment, and Napoleon, who was crowned emperor in 1804, refused to give him either the back pay that he was due or a pension. In the last months of his life, Dumas went to Paris to ask the emperor for justice, but his former colleague would not even see him. Other old friends, fearing Napoleon's displeasure, also let him down. In 1806, Thomas–Alexandre returned to Villers–Cotterets to die. On his deathbed he is said to have asked God why he, who had commanded three armies at the age of thirty–five, should die in bed at forty "like a coward," leaving his wife and his children.[27] When he died, his daughter, Aimée, was thirteen years old; Alexandre was only four. The character Haydée in his novel *The Count of Monte Cristo* is supposed to have been the same age as Alexandre was when her father died. She states in chapter 86 of that book that four is not too young to remember "events that have . . . supreme importance."[28]

It seems as though she speaks for Dumas here, for in his own life this was also the case. All his life he remembered the general, and his admiration of the heroic figure of his father amounted to hero worship. It showed in little things—like his father he had a West Indian accent (although born and brought up in France)[29]—and in big things—Dumas tried to emulate the general's military feats whenever possible, involving himself eagerly in the fighting whenever there were liberal uprisings in France. He kept his father's memory alive; telling his own children his memories of Thomas–Alexandre and contributing money to raise a statue of the general in Haiti at the request of a delegation from the homeland.[30] He wrote about the general continually. A large proportion of his three thousand–page memoirs (written in 1850) concern his father's rather than his own life. His father haunted his fiction as well. The general may be found in heroic figures like Dumas' three musketeers, who routinely do the impossible;

they are clearly based on the man who could hold off an army single handedly and do chin-ups in the stables, lifting his horse off the ground with his powerful thighs.[31] The theme of ingratitude that runs through Dumas' work, showing that those who do great things are not always greatly rewarded, was certainly based, too, on what he saw in his father's life. "I adored my father," he wrote in *Mémoires*, "even today the remembrance of . . . [him,] . . . each curve of his body and each feature of his face, is as present for me as if I had lost him yesterday; so much so that today I love him still, I love him with a love as tender, as profound and as real as if he had watched over my youth and as if I had had the happiness to pass from youth to adolescence leaning on his powerful arm."[32] It is clear that any serious study of Dumas must take into account this great influence on his life.

Writing to his former comrade General Brune in 1802, Thomas-Alexandre described his daughter Aimée as having "little black fingers."[33] Her famous brother could not have been described in the same way. He wrote in his memoirs that his mother had been afraid that he would be born black. She had seen a puppet show version of Faust while she was pregnant, and had been terrified, thinking that her baby, like the devil depicted there, might be the color of coal, "with a scarlet tongue and tail," a "throwback."[34] She began to call her unborn son "Berlick," the name of that devil, while he was still in the womb; when she saw his dark, newborn face, she screamed and fainted.[35] Alexandre's dark color at birth, though, was due to his having half-strangled on his umbilical cord. When he was able to breathe, his complexion cleared and it could be seen that he was blond and fair-skinned.[36] He did not keep these looks, however. Had Mme. Dumas known a black woman who was a mother, she might have been told that it was not likely that he would. Most black children are not born with the complexion they keep for life; darkness comes gradually. Marie-Cessette's grandson would always have blue eyes. But his blond hair changed in color and took on a frizzy texture; and his skin also changed. Photographs of him as a man show someone who, though pale for a black person, could never have been mistaken for white. In the United States he would have been considered "yellow" (or "high yellow"), "light-skinned" but most definitely a Negro. Dumas in the United States, in the nineteenth century . . . the idea is difficult to imagine. He considered doing a lecture tour here, towards the end of his life, when he was very famous, his novels well known and respected, but he questioned whether "we had sufficiently conquered our negrophobia" to be able to receive him "as he is accustomed to be received in France."[37] It was an intelligent question. The year was 1864; the Emancipation Proclamation had already been given, although it would not be enforced in the rebellious South for another year, and blacks there would not be granted all the legal rights whites had until the 1960s. Dumas never did make this tour, so we cannot tell how he actually would have been received. A very famous foreigner, although black, might have been treated with some minimum of respect. The author of The Three Musketeers probably would not have been chased through the streets with crowds threatening to lynch him and his publishers (although this did happen to one nineteenth-century black composer who dared have his works performed in public, incredible as it may seem). The fact that Dumas was foreign accounts for the fact that his works had been translated and published in the United States, although not those works that discussed the troubles of blacks. He knew nothing of the struggles that contemporary American blacks faced when they wanted to publish books other than slave narratives, struggles we can read about in the lives of William Wells Brown, Harriet E. Wilson, Martin R. Delaney, Frank J. Webb.

These pioneer African-American novelists were lucky to know how to read and write. It was illegal to teach blacks to read in many states, and it could be hazardous even where it was legal, as Bronson Alcott learned when his school in Massachusetts was forced to close because he admitted a little black girl in 1839.[38] Even in the twentieth century, the author Richard Wright has described the stratagems he was forced to adopt in order to use the public library, since blacks in the southern states where he lived were not eligible for library cards.[39] It is probable that Dumas would not have been a novelist if he had been born in America; it is certain that he would not have written the same sort of books. But, of course, he would not have been born here—at least not with the same parents. His father probably could not have married his mother: it was most unusual for a white woman in the United States in the nineteenth century to have relations with a black.[40] And the general himself was a phenomenon that could not have occurred in the United States. Although a mulatto here was more likely to be freed than a full-blooded black, most mulattoes remained in slavery. Careers in the military were not open even to free colored men. We had a segregated army until the Korean War, and black troops fought under white officers (when they were allowed to fight). There were no black American generals until very recent times.

It is dangerous, though, to concentrate too much on the ways in which France in the last century (and even this century) was more congenial than the United States for blacks. This gives rise to a fallacy that is still common, the sort of thinking that assumes that "better" means "perfect," leading generations of African–Americans to believe that France is a haven completely free of racism, that being black there has no effect on a person's life. This very strong myth (fed in our own century by the large number of eminent blacks who have been expatriates and formed a community in Paris[41]) is partly responsible, in Dumas' case, I think, for the obscurity in which his work on African concerns has been allowed to rest. We have seen already how his father had to combat racism in

France all his life. That Dumas himself also struggled with it is a fact that is very well documented.

His mother was very well satisfied with him once it turned out that he was not "Berlick." Their loving relationship is carefully described in *Mémoires*. He was a beloved member of a loving family—white grandparents, cousins, uncles, and aunts all completely accepting him (and his sister); he also never lacked for friends. These friends, though, could make it clear at times that they remembered that he was a different color. "You Negroes are all the same; you love glass beads and toys," Charles Nodier is known to have said to the writer, when he chose to buy, and wear, a great deal of gold jewelry after his first financial success.[42] Nodier, an eminent man of letters, respected Dumas and was responsible for the younger man's having had that success in writing. He introduced him to the producer who put on Dumas' first popular "serious" play. He certainly did not wish to hurt Dumas' feelings.

But the black man had enemies and people who were jealous of him, who were less kind. "That coon," is what Honoré de Balzac openly used to call him [43] (Balzac's own novels, so famous now, did not, in his own time, sell well.) The classic actress Mlle. Mars, who performed in many of Dumas' important plays, disliked Dumas because he belonged to the Romantic school of writers as well as for his color. "Open the windows," she used to demand after he left the room, pretending that she could distinguish an offensive Negro smell.[44] The poet Paul Verlaine labeled an older Dumas "Uncle Tom" in a triolet he wrote after photographs of Dumas appeared in 1866 that showed him in controversial poses with a white American actress from the South, Adah Isaacs Menken. Miss Mencken was called "Miss Adah" in the poem. The reference was to the little white girl, Eva, and the old black slave, Tom, in Harriet Beecher Stowe's then popular novel, *Uncle Tom's Cabin*.[45] Most of Paris got the joke. They also laughed when popular report had the writer's son saying, "My father is so vain that he is capable of mounting behind his own carriage, if only to make people think that he keeps a black servant."[46] The caricaturist Cham also knew that he would amuse when he depicted Dumas in the guise of an African cannibal, stirring a pot full of characters dressed in historical costumes (a reference to the writer's historical works).[47]

No one seriously thought Dumas was a cannibal, of course, but on at least one occasion the writer's color *did* arouse fear. During the July Revolution of 1830, Lafayette (the same man who had fought in the Revolutionary War in the United States) sent Dumas, who took an active part in this uprising, with orders to get ammunition from a powder magazine for the use of the men on the barricades who were trying to overthrow the government of Charles X. (Lafayette, by the way, had been shocked when he returned to the United States a few years earlier and saw the position of the blacks there. He told Thomas Jefferson frankly that such conditions did not concur with the ideas of equality for which he, for one, had fought.)[48] Dumas went to Soissons where the Commandant who held the powder magazine did not want to give up the ammunition. The man's wife, Mme. de Linières, who had lived through the revolution in Haiti in the 1790s, came in, and when she saw Dumas, a black man with guns in his hands, she began screaming hysterically. "Give up, give up, it's the second revolution of the Negroes," she told her husband, demanding that he surrender.[49] Dumas got his ammunition; no one could calm the woman down without that. This incident has its amusing side, but Dumas did not laugh when he campaigned for public office in the Yonne *departement* a decade later and was heckled as a "marquis" (a reference to the Davy de la Pailleterie title) and as a "nigger."[50] He could beat the voter who made these remarks (and did), but he did not win the election; though Victor Hugo, his colleague, friend, and rival, won a similar one. Perhaps he should run for office in the West Indies, he bitterly remarked, saying that the people there would accept him as "one of them," if he sent a lock of his kinky hair.[51]

Some would say, perhaps, that these events and remarks were isolated incidents in what was basically a life full of success and extraordinary adulation. The fact that Dumas was black, after all, did not stop him from becoming a famous playwright, ranked with Victor Hugo and Lamartine; he still cannot be ignored when discussing the history of the Romantic drama in France. Nor did it stop him from changing careers when the classic theatre became popular again, making himself into *the* most successful writer of serial novels in the great age of serial writing in France, so famous that editors could (and did) sell anything, written by him or not, at fantastic prices when it was signed with his name. Nor did it stop him from being so idolized by the public that after performances of his plays people fought to touch him, ripping his clothes to shreds for souvenirs, behavior that is matched in our time only by fans at rock concerts.[52] Being black did not stop him from associating, on equal terms, with the other great writers during that great age of literature in France. Hugo, Georges Sand, Alphonse Lamartine, Alfred-Victor de Vigny were all acquaintances, many were close friends; younger writers like the Goncourt brothers were honored just to meet him.[53] He was on intimate terms with French royalty, in spite of his known republican opinions, and enjoyed the patronage of the house of Orléans. He traveled all over Europe, went to Russia, the Middle East, and North Africa—often as the honored guest of potentates and kings. There is a story someone told about going to a royal party in Spain, and seeing the king, queen, and princess left alone in a corner while the guests all gathered around one man: it was, of course, Dumas, famed for his wit and brilliant conversation.[54] Giuseppe Garibaldi called him "tu." He collected honors and military decorations. He became wealthy enough to indulge his fantasies, building the spectacular, ostentatious castle

Monte Cristo, named after his famous novel, and buying a yacht, like the count in that book.

And then there were the love affairs. Even after he lost the considerable good looks he had as a youth and became grey, elderly, and fat, he continued to attract some of the most famous beauties of his time. His famous son, his namesake (he had four children by four different women, the last when he was a very old man), complained that most of the women he met just wanted to be introduced to his father. He once was heard to complain in public that the old man gave him his shoes to break in when they were new and his mistresses when he was tired of them.[55] Despite some disappointments (he never was admitted to the Académie Française, an honor he coveted), and despite the fact that he was so careless with money that he ended up poor after all the millions he made (he was cared for, in extreme old age, by his son Alexandre Dumas), Dumas led a fairy-tale life, the sort of life of which most people are only able to dream. Perhaps he was able to make the marvelous seem so real in many of his novels because it was real in his own life.

If it does seem like quibbling to say that, in spite of all this, the writer always felt like an outsider and was always aware of his skin color, I can only offer the excuse that it was certainly true. Some remarks he made suggest that he, at times, felt inferior because of it. He once said to the actress Marie Dorval, comparing himself to de Vigny, that the other writer was a "true nobleman," not "a mulatto like myself."[56] He also told one of his black servants (throughout his life, he employed many blacks), who was leaving to go into the army, that if he made good there "everyone will swear you are white."[57] This kind of thinking was hardly to be avoided considering the society in which he lived. After all, one of the first lessons he ever learned was that "Berlick" would not have been worthy of the love even of the woman who bore him.

It is not remarkable that Dumas had these thoughts sometimes. What *is* remarkable is that he never tried to hide or obscure his heritage; that he wrote about slavery and the injustices done to blacks when these were things that did not concern him personally or affect his life; that he tried to portray the blacks in his works as human beings, not stereotypes, when he had no models for this kind of thinking in the books he read and no idea how to go about doing it; and that he interested himself in the freedom of blacks in foreign countries and tried to do what he could for them. He was interested in freedom and equality for everyone, of course. He put his life at risk on the barricades in France, for instance, and donated time and money to Garibaldi's cause in Italy. But most liberals in his time cared about those causes. It was stylish to do so. It was *not* stylish, however, to write after he visited Africa (Tangier) in 1846 that he "felt the Moroccan scorn and hatred for the European invader."[58] He swam completely against French public opinion when he took the side of the North against the South during the American Civil War, trying to find a newspaper "willing to open a subscription to help" the Union's sick and wounded. He could not. He then proposed to write a history of the first four years of Abraham Lincoln's presidency, to refute the idea, popular in England as well as in France, that "the North intends not so much the freedom of the blacks as the oppression of the whites."[59] This project also fell through. But he tried. He does not deserve to have it believed of him that he was untouched by and did not care about the concerns of his people, because it's convenient, in order to sell *The Three Musketeers*, to suppress his political side.

Dumas died on December 5, 1870. Paris was occupied by the Germans at that time, and his funeral was not well attended. But when he was reinterred after the troubles were over at Villers–Cotterets, his birthplace, the eulogies the great spoke over him were such as any man might envy. His real and most lasting eulogy, though, is the popularity of his books, which people have never ceased to read from his time until our own, all over the world. He was the greatest of the three great Dumas.

However, it was Alexandre Dumas *fils*, his son, who was thought to be the greatest of his illustrious family in his own time. For the whole of the last part of the nineteenth century after Hugo's death, he was indisputably the preeminent man of letters in France. He received honors that his father never dreamed of, including election to the prestigious Académie, becoming one of the "forty immortals." It is ironic that today he is considered a one–book author, and that that book, *La Dame aux Camélias* [*Camille*], is best known through Giuseppe Verdi's music as *La Traviata*.

Armand Duval, the hero of *Camille* (Verdi changed his name to Alfredo), has never, to my knowledge, been portrayed as black. Yet it was common knowledge that Dumas *fils* based his hero on himself and that the 1847 novel, and the later 1852 play, were very thinly disguised autobiography. It is amusing to compare the grave and respectable M. Duval, Armand's father, with the bohemian elder Dumas, but most of the other characters in the work are supposed to be exact portraits, especially Marguerite, based on the beautiful courtesan Marie Duplessis, who died shortly before the young man wrote the novel at age twenty–four. The story told in it was true to the point that Dumas reproduced, word for word, actual correspondence between himself and his lover.[60]

He does not seem to have had the imagination that his father had. Many of his other works were also based on his own experiences: *Diane de Lys*, for example, on another love affair; *Le Fils Naturel* [*The Illegitimate Son*], though more loosely, on his problematic relationship with his father. When he was not writing disguised autobiography, he wrote plays about the social problems of his time. They were very well done, and it is not surprising that his contemporaries ranked him so highly as an author. Yet, the social problems that he wrote about have largely disappeared (and even in his own time, only concerned a small, elite segment of the population), the wit he was famed for was based on topical references that mean nothing to us now, and to the reader of today his plays are not very interesting. He would probably be known only as the son of his father were it not for his book about Marguerite Gautier. The kind of youthful emotion he describes in *Camille* (which is not sentimental, like *La Traviata*) is still understandable even today, when there are no longer any courtesans and when people no longer sacrifice themselves for love.

Dumas *fils* never wrote anything dealing with the concerns of blacks; it seems not to have been one of the social problems that interested him. In his own life, the stigma of illegitimacy bothered him a great deal more than his being a person of color. He was not black in appearance, as photographs of him clearly show. Armand Duval is "a tall, pale young man with blond hair"; so was Dumas *fils*.[61] It seems, at first glance, that he lived as a white man. Although he wrote about questions that concerned the bourgeoisie, he was not middle class in later life but lived among the aristocracy, married a Russian princess, and was wealthy, eminent, and respected, as well as a member of the Académie. It is rather a shock to find among the opinions the *Mercure de France* collected about him after his death (opinions that were mostly adulatory) such remarks as Léon Bloy's "that mulatto. . . was a fool and a hypocrite," and Adrien Remacle's "this Frenchman, a little bit negro, born clever [*malin*], created a morality of facade and preface."[62] And then one finds that, during his life, he took pride in his black ancestry, although it no longer showed in face or feature, or in the color of his skin. At the height of his fame, in 1887, when Léon Ganderax wished to please Dumas *fils* and compliment him, he could find no way more sure of doing it than by referring to his African origins. Ganderax called the eminent man "an admirable Negro" and said that he had "the temperament of a Negro" combined with "the highest degree of sharp-edged reasoning." And he finished by saying that Dumas *fils* was a worthy grandson of Thomas-Alexandre Dumas, the General, "the hero of Brixen."[63]

II. *Alexandre Dumas: Black Writer, French Writer*

When Dumas *père* gave his son, who wanted to be a writer, too, a list of authors to read, he recommended Virgil, Horace, Homer, Sophocles, and Euripides in the original Latin and Greek. He also thought that the young man should read Shakespeare, Dante, Schiller, and the Bible—and learn Corneille by heart. The contemporaries, or near contemporaries, that he recommended were André-Marie de Chénier, Hugo and Lamartine.[64] This list differed somewhat from the list that he had been given, as a young man beginning to write literature, of authors that *he* should read. Besides the authors on the list quoted above, he had also been recommended to familiarize himself with Aeschylus and Aristophanes; Seneca, Terence, and Plautus; Molière, Racine, Voltaire. He had been told to read Goethe, Walter Scott, James Fenimore Cooper, Ronsard, Milton, Byron, Johann Uhland, and Mathurin Régnier, and to familiarize himself with the history of France, through the classic authors like Jean de Joinville, Jean Froissart, the Count of Saint-Simon, and Mme. de la Fayette Richelieu.[65] He gives this list in his *Memoirs* but does not say how many of these authors he actually read, except to say that he was powerfully influenced by Scott, Cooper, and Byron.

Dumas needed a list of authors to read because he had very little formal education. As the son of the disgraced General Dumas, growing up during the period when Napoleon was in power, Dumas was denied a scholarship to either a *lycée* or a military school and his mother had had no money to send him. She was the only widow of a Revolutionary general who did not receive a pension, and the family was always close to dire poverty, since a woman in those days really could not support herself. She managed to obtain lessons for Alexandre with Abbé Grégoire, the village priest, where he learned "a little Latin, a little grammar"[66] and developed a very beautiful, rapid handwriting, which later stood him in good stead. He learned dancing, fencing, and how to fire a pistol (not with the priest), but he could not, or would not, learn arithmetic beyond multiplication. This was very possibly the reason that he proved to be so bad at handling his financial affairs in later life. His mother arranged for him to take music lessons (his sister sang beautifully and she wanted him to have this advantage, too), but he had "the worst voice in the world."[67] His mother wanted him to become a priest and actually had the chance to send him to a seminary, but the young boy ran away from this opportunity, like Aramis in *The Three Musketeers*.[68] His mother tried other careers for him, but he wasn't successful at any of them, until a 1819 performance of *Hamlet* (not the original, but Jean–François Ducis' French translation) inspired him to begin to write for the theatre, a decision in which he was encouraged by his friend Adolphe de Leuven.[69]

One notices at once that there were no black authors in the list of books that Dumas read. Of course, he was not familiar with any. He grew up and basically lived all his life in a vacuum as far as contact with blacks was concerned, although there were blacks writing during his lifetime. Within a few generations after the slave ships first landed in the New World, the transplanted Africans, though they had come from an oral culture like Homer's, had taken up the European's pen and begun to write about their experiences—in spite of the fact that they were given little encouragement to do so. The true explosion of slave narratives occurred during the nineteenth century in the United States, but Gustavus Vassa (Olaudah Equiano) (1745-97) in England and others wrote about their experiences before Dumas was born. Phillis Wheatley (1753–84) and Jupiter Hammon (1720–1800) wrote poetry in the New World. Benjamin Banneker (1731–1806), famous for other reasons, also wrote verse. In spite of adverse conditions, as we saw in the previous chapter, blacks like George Moses Horton, James M. Whitfield, and Frances Watkins Harper in America would write novels and poems during Dumas' lifetime as well. The United States was not the only country where blacks were writing. Auguste Lacaussade, another black Frenchman, born in 1817, was honored by the Académie for his poems, received the Prix Bordin in 1852, and was elected to membership in the Legion d' honueur in 1860.[70] Maria F. dos Reis published a novel in Brazil in 1859. And in Russia, where the conditions were not adverse, a young man of mixed black and white aristocratic ancestry like Dumas, the Frenchman's almost exact contemporary, was trying, during Dumas' lifetime, to write about *his* black experience, about his ancestors and his feelings about his race. This was, of course, Alexander Pushkin, most notably in his unfinished novel, *The Negro of Peter the Great*.[71] Dumas would never read this book.[72] He never traveled to the United States or Brazil, and when he went to Russia in his later years, Pushkin (who was murdered when he was thirty–seven years old) was long dead. So when the French author tried to read about the obvious difference between himself and his friends, family, lovers, compatriots, when he tried to find out about people who looked like him, he was forced to dig for morsels in the only literature with which he had any familiarity: the "classics"—literature by whites.

That any work with black characters fascinated him from the beginning is obvious. *Hamlet* was the first of Shakespeare's works to which he was introduced and, as mentioned before, he liked it so much that it inspired him to begin to write. But *Othello* had an even greater effect on him. Describing his reactions to the play about the Moor of Venice (probably the most famous work in Western literature whose hero is black), he would later say that it struck him as if he had been "a man born blind to whom sight is then given" and said that the performance opened an "enchanted Eden . . . for me."[73]

His own first piece of theatrical writing (with Adolphe de Leuven as a collaborator) was *Pélérinage à Ermenonville* [*Pilgrimage to Ermenonville*]. A half–verse, half–prose "pastiche of Demoustier" is how he later described it, in *Mémoires*.[74] He went on to do some work in the vaudeville theatre, because he needed money. Some of these plays survive, but the first *serious* work that he tried was a translation of Schiller's *Die Vershwörung des Fiesko zu Genua* [*The Conspiracy of Fiesco at Genoa*]. This play, written by Schiller in 1783, has a Moor, Muley Hassan, as one of the main characters. He is a villain, Fiesco's tool in his plots against the Doria family. Dumas, who did an adaptation of the play rather than an exact translation, felt that it was important that it be recognized that Hassan was black. In his memoirs, he expressed anger at other translators of the play (which was very popular during the Romantic period) who suppressed the character of the moor or made him white.[75] His translation, *Fiesques de Lavagna*, made in 1823, was never performed and never published. Dumas later claimed that he burnt the manuscript, but it still exists. The play had a great effect on him: it is mentioned in *Monte Cristo* and was one of the influences on the writing of *Charles VII chez ses grands vassaux*.

It was for *Charles VII* that Dumas first created a major, original character who was black. Yacoub, the slave who is the hero of this play, will be discussed at length in the next section. The play was written in 1831, after Dumas had managed to become famous, along with works that had nothing to do with anything of special concern to blacks: the great Romantic plays *Christine*, *Antony*, and *Henri III et sa cour* [*Henry III and His Court*]. Although these plays are largely unknown in the United States, they are what his reputation as a major writer rests on today in France. These plays dealt with

Dumas' other interests: In *Henri III*, he first showed his talent for dramatizing the history of France. He would always care a great deal about the history of his country and was instrumental in bringing it to the attention of the common man. In *Antony*, he achieved the revolutionary feat of setting a story about a difficult subject (adultery) in contemporary times, with real people, a story that, although melodramatic, was also realistic. One critic said that "Dumas gave evidence of early naturalistic tendencies by assigning his hero's character to the unhappy circumstances of his childhood as a foundling," a kind of character development that was unique when he wrote the play.[76] Antony, a "rebel and a bastard,"[77] was the first of Dumas' many "outsider" heroes. The play *Christine*, about Queen Christina of Sweden and the murder of Monaldeschi, first takes up the theme of ingratitude that Dumas would use in many of his novels (including the Musketeer series), particularly the ingratitude of the great. These plays were all fantastically successful. *Henri III and His Court* was the first Romantic play ever to be performed (although Hugo's *Cromwell* was written first), and *Antony* made Dumas famous all over France. *Charles VII*, though not a failure, did not have this kind of spectacular success. None of the other plays that Dumas wrote during the 1830s (his most prolific period of dramatic writing) dealt with themes of specific interest to blacks. The most important of the works he wrote during this period are *The Tower of Nesle* (1832), still his most often performed work, which is a reworking of a play by Frédéric Gaillardet dealing with sex, intrigue, and murder in high places in medieval Paris; *Kean, or Disorder and Genius*, written in 1836, based on the life of the British actor Edmund Kean, famous for both his thespian skill and his dissolute, drunken life; and *Mademoiselle de Belle-Isle* (1839), a comedy of manners, set in eighteenth-century France.

Dumas' interests as a writer were varied. At no time did he feel, as black authors in the United States today are often made to feel, that only certain subjects were suitable for him to write about because he was black. The literature of the world has been greatly enriched because of the breadth of Dumas' interests. He felt free not only to try out different subject matter but different genres as well. When there was a reaction in favor of the classic drama in the 1840s,[78] he began to try to write novels, although he had only written plays previously. Novels translate more easily than plays do, especially plays in verse, and it is as a novelist that Dumas is best known today outside of France. Works like *The Three Musketeers*, *The Count of Monte Cristo*, *The Black Tulip*, *The Queen's Necklace*, *Ange Pitou* (*Storming the Bastille*), *The Countess of Charny*, *Twenty Years After*, *Chicot the Jester* (*La Dame de Monsoreau*), *Le Vicomte de Bragelonne* (which includes *The Man in the Iron Mask*) need little introduction to the English-speaking reader. Dumas also wrote cookbooks and children's books and he continued to translate. His version of Hoffmann's *The Nutcracker and the Mouse King*, which he called *La Casse-Noisette*, not the original, is the basis of Tchaikovsky's well-known ballet. He was well regarded as a travel writer,[79] wrote his memoirs, and founded two newspapers at different times of his life. If he never felt limited in subject matter or genre because he was black, a certain sensibility that can be attributed to his identity as a person of color *does* pervade much of his work. It is found in two recurrent themes in his fiction, the theme of the "outsider" and the theme of revenge.

Perhaps it is best to consider these themes first as they are presented in *Georges* (1843), one of Dumas' forgotten novels, and one of his most important, as it is the author's only novel in which the hero is black. Georges Munier is a "half-caste," the son of a mulatto father (as Dumas was), who lived on the island of Mauritius (formerly called Ile-de-France) near Africa, east of Madagascar in the Indian Ocean. Dumas never visited there, but he learned about it from a friend, Felicien Malleville, who grew up there.[80] Georges' color makes him unacceptable to the white planter society to which he aspires to belong; he's an outsider, an outcast. When he is insulted by a white man in one of the novel's key scenes, he cannot challenge the person who has offended him to a duel because a black man cannot strike a white man on Mauritius (just as in Sainte–Domingue, in Thomas–Alexandre's time, blacks there are outside of the code of honor that "gentlemen" live by). Georges goes away to live in Paris and returns to his island years later—wealthy, erudite, cosmopolitan. Still not accepted by the whites, he takes revenge on them by forming a slave rebellion, joining with the blacks that many other mulattoes despise. He also gains the love of the woman who was betrothed to the white man who had formerly offended him.[81]

At the beginning of this century, Frances Miltoun characterized *Georges* as "an autobiographical novel." It could only have been written, she claimed, by someone who, because of race, caste, or religion saw himself unfairly outclassed by his contemporaries.[82] *Georges* is not autobiographical in the way that *Ange Pitou* (*Storming the Bastille*) is autobiographical: in the latter novel, Dumas made the hero a boy from Villers–Cotterets and put many of his own experiences into it, although he set it in the time of the Revolution. But *Georges* certainly deals with feelings that Dumas seems to have felt. Although he was considered a gentleman and fought several duels, he could not call someone to account every time his color was called to his attention, and he did not. He was known as a good–natured man, but he seems to have experienced hostile feelings nonetheless: the kind of feelings that caused him to suspend the man who insulted him in Yonne over a bridge until he took the insult back, the kind of feelings that explain the revision of the story about Thomas–Alexandre in the theatre so that the black man got revenge for the slight.

The Count of Monte Cristo is, of course, Dumas' great novel about vengeance—"probably the greatest revenge novel ever written" says one critic.[83] It is not about white and black relations, though Dumas put long, passionate speeches about freedom into the mouth of the white slave Haydee,[84] but the plot is so similar to the plot of *Georges* that a comparison of the two books would be worthwhile. In *Monte Cristo*, which is, astonishingly enough, based on a true life story,[85] Dumas seems to be questioning by the end of the book whether vengeance is ultimately worthwhile even for the greatest wrong. Edmond Dantès at first thinks himself the instrument of God, but he eventually wonders whether he has gone too far when the innocent and even those he wants to reward begin to be affected by the train of events he sets in motion as he seeks his revenge. In *Le Vicomte de Bragelonne*, one of the sequels to *The Three Musketeers*, Athos, the most thoughtful of the musketeers, asks the same question when Milady's son begins to hunt down the musketeers for the murder of his mother, an act they thought was a just act of vengeance when they committed it. The question is abstract here and does not seem to have anything to do with race relations, but in *Charles VII*, it is clearly a racial question when Yacoub seeks vengeance on the men who captured him and stole his freedom. It is worth noting, though, that even Yacoub hesitates over whether the kindnesses the Count has done him are not sufficient to atone for his wrongs; and the question seems to be one about which Dumas was ambivalent.

Dantès, Georges, Yacoub, Antony, and other of Dumas' characters who seek vengeance have another trait in common: they are all different from the people around them, as Dumas was different from the people among whom he lived in real life. In the beginning of the novel of which he is the hero, Dantès is happy and well-adjusted in his society—a handsome, young, soon-to-be-married sailor of nineteen who is successful at his job and about to receive a promotion. But when he is reborn as the Count of Monte Cristo, after his long imprisonment and equally long travels, he is so different from his fellows that some of them question, half-jokingly, whether he is even human. There is a long section in which they consider that he might be a vampire. And he is able to associate with people that he knew intimately in former days completely unrecognized. There's no touch of the supernatural about the young man from Gascony, D'Artagnan, but at the beginning of the novel about him, he's also on the outside. Worse than that, he's ridiculous. *The Three Musketeers* begins with a scene in which everyone in the whole town of Meung laughs at him and his horse as he rides into town; he literally causes a riot. He later makes himself ridiculous again to Porthos, Athos, and Aramis, the three men whom he most wishes to impress, and even after he is accepted by them, they continue to remind him periodically that he is a Gascon, with different mannerisms and a different accent. Ange Pitou, in *Storming the Bastille*, doesn't fit in at first because he is a country bumpkin from Dumas' home town of Villers–Coterrets; Marie Antoinette in the French Revolution novels is continually reminded that she is not French but Austrian; the man in the iron mask has been excluded since birth from his rightful place as the king's son and from all human society, even before he's forced to wear the cage on his face that marks him like Cain. It's very easy to make a long list of Dumas characters who are on the outside, a theme in his novels that would make an interesting study.

Much remains to be studied critically in Dumas' novels and plays. His work has never received the critical attention that it deserves. One of the most popular authors of all time, he has not been considered to rank with the most significant, especially not in this country. There are several reasons for this, I think. His very popularity is a mark against him. Writers whose works are enjoyable to read often have to struggle against the kind of critical prejudice that assumes "significant" means "dull." The fact that Dumas is such a fine storyteller has been held against him. Most people also probably first read him when they are young (his books are most easily found in libraries in the "juvenile" section) and assume, when they are older, that there is nothing more to him than what they understood when they were fifteen years of age.

Dumas' life was so colorful and flamboyant, too, that the critics who want to study him tend to get sidetracked in discussing his duels and mistresses rather than his work. I was able to find many biographies when researching this essay, but not many critical studies, especially not recent ones. There are other problems, too. Dumas was certainly an overly prolific writer. As the author (sometimes with collaborators) of over seven hundred works, he was often repetitive, and sometimes wrote things that were just plain bad; it is difficult to sort through all his books and impossible to read all of them. And then there is the question of the collaborators. The question "Exactly how much of the works of Dumas did Dumas actually write?" has been asked ever since Jean–Baptiste Jacquot, writing under the pseudonym Eugene de Mirecourt, published the scurrilous pamphlet *Fabrique de Romans, Alexandre Dumas & Cie*. [*Alexander Dumas & Co., Novel Factory*].[86] That Mirecourt was discredited in a court of a law because of this pamphlet, condemned to fifteen days in prison, forced to make a retraction, and later was proved to be a plagiarist himself has not seemed to matter; the mud still sticks.[87] This has happened even though when Dumas is known to have used a collaborator (the most important of these was Auguste Maquet), evidence exists showing who wrote which part of the books. Maquet was responsible for parts of the Musketeer novels and of *Monte Cristo*, but a court ruled that he had not done enough work on any of these books to be listed as co-author. Maquet wrote novels on his own as well, but none of them is any good.[88]

Bad translators have done more harm to Dumas in the English–speaking world than Mirecourt and Maquet, unfortunately. That Aramis should be called a "stout" young man in the most readily available translation of *The Three Musketeers* is bad enough.[89] Dumas actually wrote only that he was young, (Dumas wrote nothing about his size), but Dumas' language very often is rendered carelessly and imprecisely, in the mistaken idea that only the story counts with him. This makes it impossible to do many kinds of critical studies of his work. His works have also frequently been abridged in the most careless way, so that one has no sense, when reading his works in English, of the careful way that he plotted them in French.

The Man in the Iron Mask is the worst example of poor cutting. This book actually does not exist in French, since the English work with this name is a compilation of excerpts from several works, chopped up and pasted back together. Although it is an exciting story, it is no longer a work of literature but simply hash.[90] The edition of the *Count of Monte Cristo* that is easiest to find today is not quite so bad, but it has also been mercilessly cut — only about a quarter of the work has actually been translated. From what is left (though it is translated competently enough), it is impossible to see why Dickens and others so admired the novel. The careful plotting, the point and counterpoint of the great themes of revenge, resurrection, man's right to play God, mercy, and marriage (not to speak of the slavery theme) are no longer there; nothing remains except a simple story line.

Georges is Dumas' only work with a black theme that has ever been translated into English — and this was not done until 1975, one hundred and twenty-two years after it was first published. I have not found any translations of *Fiesques*, and *Charles VII chez ses grands vassaux* has never, until now, been published in the United States.

III. *King Charles VII and Yacoub the Slave*

Charles VII chez ses grands vassaux was written in the summer of 1831. After the success of *Antony*, Dumas went to the Trouville in the company of Belle Krelsamer, his latest mistress. On the quiet beach there he wrote rapidly, finishing his five-act drama in little more than a month, at the rate of a hundred lines a day.[91] The play had been contracted by his producer, Harel, and when he returned to Paris it was put into production. It was first performed at the Odéon Theatre on October 21, 1831; the text of the play was also first published that year. Dumas was proud of the play at first. He posed for a portrait wearing Yacoub's costume[92] and went to a lot of trouble to make the play successful, even shooting and stuffing a deer for a prop needed in act 1 when Harel refused to go to the expense. But the play was not a success, at least not by Dumas' standards. I have already described the adulation to which he had become accustomed after the performances of *Henri III*, *Christine*, and *Antony*. He was to receive this sort of mad acclaim again for *Richard Darlington*, performed later the same year, but *Charles VII* left the audience "cold." Antoine Fontaney observed in his diary that the "the play is not as good as Dumas' plays usually are."[93] Later critics have sometimes agreed. André Maurois called *Charles VII* "quite valueless, except for some . . . fine declamatory passages on the subject of race prejudice, a problem which touched Dumas to the quick."[94] And Dumas, who valued popularity, later came to underrate the play himself.[95]

The actors had thought enough of the play to fight for parts when Dumas first presented it to them, though,[96] and it was very successful when revived later in the nineteenth century.[97] Hippolyte Parigot, an important nineteenth-century critic of Dumas' plays, admired *Charles VII* a great deal, saying that it was the author's best play in verse.[98] And Alexandre Dumas *fils*, himself a major playwright, once observed that he would rather have "written *Charles VII*, which did not succeed" than any of his own very popular works.[99]

Whatever one thinks of the play, it is a landmark, without a doubt, in the history of literature written by diaspora Africans. As I mentioned in the last section, *Charles VII* was not the first poetry written in a European language by a black; however it does contain some of the earliest lines written pro-

testing the slave trade, and some of the most eloquent. Where
Phillis Wheatley had been content to write "Twas mercy
brought me from my pagan land," and Jupiter Hammon had
agreed, "God's tender mercy brought thee here,"[100] Dumas'
Yacoub observes, in perfect, classic alexandrines:

> . . what have I done that I should suffer like this? . . .
> Oh—if some tribal chieftain on the shores of the Nile came
> into the bosom of your family, woman, where everything
> was thriving, and took your son or father from you . . . if
> they treated him over there the way that I'm treated here;
> if they put a collar like this around his neck—you would un-
> derstand that hatred doesn't go back into the soul as easily
> as this blade into this sheath![101]

These lines ring out, even today. How much more powerful they must have been in 1831, when black slavery was still
legal in Latin America and the West Indies as well as in the
United States, when the kind of kidnapping that Yacoub
describes was a daily occurrence. Even those, like Maurois,
who don't admire the play, admit that Yacoub's speeches are
very fine. Dumas was not a first-class poet; he could not hope
to rank with Victor Hugo, for instance, when it came to writing verse, and he knew it. He also knew that he had exceeded
his usual standard with Yacoub and said in his memoirs that
some of the slave's speeches "rank among the few really good
lines of poetry that I have written."[102] It is not only the words
that Yacoub speaks that stand out; the Saracen stands out as
a character, an original and fascinating creation.

It is interesting to compare Yacoub with the most famous
black in Western literature—Othello. Fontaney called *Charles
VII* "a kind of *Othello* turned inside out"[103] and Dumas admitted that Shakespeare's Moor was one of the prototypes for the
character.[104] Both Dumas' and Shakespeare's characters are
called "Moors," Yacoub a "Saracen." Yacoub is a slave, and
Othello has been a slave, although he is, at the time of the
play, an important Venetian general.[105] Both are living

among Europeans rather than among their own people, and both are subject to the kind of open and insulting racism that allows Barbantio to tell Othello that he has a "sooty bosom"[106] and Balthazar to taunt Yacoub as "snowball."[107] The general and the slave are also both passionately in love with European women, and the reason for their love is that the women have listened to them with sympathy: Desdemona to Othello's tales of his travels and exploits, and Berengaria to Yacoub's complaints about his troubles and his stories about his native land. Both men finally commit murder because of their love for these women against their better judgment, misguidedly listening to others' words of persuasion. Othello believes Iago's slanders and kills the object of his passion in a jealous rage; Yacoub is persuaded to kill the husband of the woman he loves by that woman herself.[108]

In spite of these similarities, though, Yacoub and Othello are not really alike in personality. Othello strikes the reader as a very courtly, noble, thoroughly assimilated Venetian nobleman, that is until Iago strips him of his superficial self-confidence and shows the uncertainty and the raw, elemental passions lurking beneath. Yacoub, however, has never been assimilated into medieval French society and does not want to be. He makes it clear that he rejects the Europeans and their mores from the beginning of Dumas' play. In his first long speech, in act 1, scene 1, Yacoub describes how he hunted down a lion in the desert, in response to the white archers' remarks that he is a "savage," that he can't know anything of hunting — "the sport of nobles; of Christians." He says to the archers derisively at the end of this speech that *they* don't understand hunting, "the sport of infidels."[109] He continues to oppose his values to European values throughout the play, insisting that his own culture is as valid, in fact more valid, than theirs. In spite of the fact that he says in act 2, scene 5, that he has no religion, he insists earlier in the play that the religion he was brought up in is equal to Christianity, and is willing to fight to insist on that.[110] He does not accept

Charles of Savoisy's right to make war in Africa and deprive Africans of their liberty, even at the command of the Pope; he doesn't care who wins the war going on in France, the English or the French; and he claims that he has the right to kill Guy-Raymond, the Count's servant, according to the laws of his native desert and gets the Count to accept that claim.[111] It is clear that Yacoub is a different type of character than Othello. And Dumas makes it clear that Yacoub's point of view has validity in this play through the use of revolutionary device. Charles VII, King of France, is introduced into the play and used as a foil for Yacoub, unusual as it was at that time, to have a king serve as a foil for a black, a slave. The parallels between the two characters are striking. Both question the social order, as Charles of Savoisy, who speaks for authority, does not; both reject the war that the other characters regard as all important, giving precedence to their personal concerns and happiness; both are convinced to do things against their principles because of their love for a woman — Yacoub kills Count Charles for Berengaria and the king goes to war only when urged to do so by Agnes Sorel. Weak King Charles is even called a "slave" by the Count of Savoisy in one very striking passage,[112] emphasizing the parallel, although he interests the reader less than the African does. It was with wonderful irony, I think, that Dumas named the play after the king, the same irony that makes the only scene (act 3, scene 3) in which the two men speak directly to each other so intriguing: Charles condescends to Yacoub, not really listening to what the slave has to say, not even noticing at first that Yacoub is present, and certainly never dreaming that the slave is of any importance, while we listen, knowing that Yacoub, not Charles, is the real hero of the play. We know that Charles is not even correct in thinking that he saved Yacoub's life, which Agnes so flatteringly gives him credit for. Berengaria, who forbade the slave to kill himself, is Yacoub's real savior.

Dumas' parallels between King Charles and Yacoub were

so original that even modern critics have failed to perceive the connection. In 1957, André Maurois could write that Charles VII and Agnes Sorel were only included in the work for "reasons of prestige."[113] The careful reader will see, though, that nothing in this play is there unnecessarily, that in spite of the speed with which Dumas wrote it, it is very thoughtfully put together indeed. Dumas' use of language is notable. Although the poetry, other than when Yacoub speaks, can be somewhat lacking (the alexandrines stumble at times in order to rhyme), the descriptions and imagery are wonderful. Who can forget the word pictures called up by "the great granite sphinx, ancient sentinel of the ancient desert" for example, or the dead Counts of Savoisy asleep "on their tombs in iron winding sheets in the glimmering of funeral torches."[114] There's the symbolism, too, especially powerful in regard to Berengaria: she's called an angel very often, but only in the first part of the play; and the antonyms of that word—devil, hell—are used very consciously too. Other words often used and worth considering are lord, children, sun, night, black, and desert as well as Charles of Savoisy's repetition of the words honor and duty. Dumas never uses language carelessly. Parigot mentions seeing rough drafts of this play and the careful revisions, each one an improvement.[115]

There are many other things that could be considered in a critical study of *Charles VII*. There's the question of duality, for instance. Why is Charles of Savoisy given the same name as King Charles? Since they represent opposite qualities, are they almost like opposite halves of the same person? Are their discussions like a man arguing with himself? The double, or *doppelgänger*, theme certainly shows up with regard to Berengaria, in act 4, where we are shown two Countesses at once (or what Yacoub thinks are two Berengarias: the good one leaving, the bad one remaining at the castle, which has become her personal hell). The one who remains is certainly different in all essentials from anything that we have seen of Berengaria's character before. One could also study the aptness of the characters' names. Surely the name Seignelais, so similar to *seigneur* or lord, was not chosen for the fictional domain of Charles of Savoisy by accident. The subtle use of puns is very evident in the French also. "Stay here, since you like it better," Charles of Savoisy says to Yacoub at one point.[116] This could also be translated as "Stay here, since you love her better," a remark that the audience, if not the Count, could appreciate.

Even the setting of the play has been carefully chosen. The Hundred Years' War is not that familiar to English speaking readers (although there's Shakespeare's *Henry V*, and everyone knows Joan of Arc), and it seems very long ago to us, but the Paris audience that first saw *Charles VII* performed would have noticed at once some correspondences between events mentioned in the play and the recent past. They too had been at war with the English and had been defeated barely twenty years before at Waterloo, as at Crécy and Agincourt. Charles of Savoisy's speech, in which he warns the king not to let the people "think, while dying, that their king has disowned them, because they may, thinking themselves released from their oath, be seized with the desire also to disown their king" was delivered in front of people who had, within the last generation, seen Louis XVI deposed and beheaded, and within the last year, seen Charles X deposed and sent into exile.[117] The chilling description in act 2, scene 3 of "nothing but murder and civil war . . . when the soldier finishes and sheathes his sword, it's the executioner's turn" was not written long after the Reign of Terror, the Vendée, and the Revolutionary Wars, which were all well within the memories of the older members of the audience.[118] Charles of Savoisy's disagreement with Yacoub, with King Charles, and with Berengaria about the public good coming before the rights of individuals was a very vital one in 1831, as were the questions Dumas raised: How important is it to keep society running smoothly, with everyone in their proper place, even if that place for some (blacks, women) is oppressive? Does the individual have any right to try to seek personal happiness or must he/she submit to what is held to be best for the common good, especially in troubled times? These questions are, I think, still valid ones today. Dumas answered such questions in his play. Yacoub is alive, triumphant, at the end of act 5. He has his freedom and is able to go home to his desert, something most enslaved Africans never achieved. This is the only ending that Marie-Cessette Dumas' grandson *could* have written, I believe, although at first glance it doesn't seem to fit the logic of the play. Cold reason demands that Yacoub be arrested for questioning by the Count's servants. Isabelle saw him strike the Count down, and he is hardly an inconspicuous person or someone that she might mistake for anyone else. The logic of a Romantic play demands that the man who has loved Berengaria hopelessly for ten years should want to die for her. But Dumas didn't write a realistic play or a Romantic play—he wrote a play about freedom.

Notes

1. André Maurois, *Les Trois Dumas* (Paris: Librairie Hachette, 1957), p. 12 and F.W. Hemmings, *Alexandre Dumas: The King of Romance* (New York: Charles Scribner's Sons, 1979), p. 5.

2. Roger Bastide, *African Civilizations in the New World*, trans. Peter Green, (New York: Harper and Row, 1971), pp. 138-45.

3. C. L. Sulzberger, *Fathers and Children: How Famous Men Were Influenced by Their Fathers* (New York: Arbor House, 1987), p. 42 and Hemmings *Alexandre Dumas*, p. 4.

4. Hemmings, *Alexandre Dumas*, p. 4.

5. Ibid., p. 5.

6. Sulzberger, *Fathers and Children*, p. 42.

7. Maurois, *Les Trois Dumas*, p. 14.

8. C. L. R. James, *The Black Jacobins: Toussaint L'Ouverture and the San Domingo Revolution*, 2nd ed. (New York: Random House, 1963), p. 38.

9. Hemmings, *Alexandre Dumas*, p. 1.

10. Claude Schopp *Alexandre Dumas: Genius of Life*, trans. A. J. Koch (New York and Toronto: Franklin Watts, 1988), p. 15.

11. Hemmings, *Alexandre Dumas*, pp. 6–7 and Maurois *Les Trois Dumas*, p. 12.

12. The affair is well documented, both in Dumas *père*'s *Mes Mémoires* and in a contemporary police report. See Hemmings, *Alexandre Dumas*, p. 213 n. 6.

13. Ibid., p. 7

14. Ibid., p. 213 n. 6.

15. Ibid., p. 7.

16. Sulzberger, *Fathers and Children*, p. 43.

17. James, *The Black Jacobins*, p. 76.

18. Sulzberger, *Fathers and Children*, p. 40.

19. Maurois, *Les Trois Dumas*, p. 19.

20. Sulzberger, *Fathers and Children*, p. 47.

21. Maurois, *Les Trois Dumas*, p.22.

22. Sulzberger, *Fathers and Children*, p. 41.

23. Maurois, *Les Trois Dumas*, p. 23.

24. James, *The Black Jacobins*, p. 365. Toussaint died in part because he was not given proper medical care, his doctor and surgeon having been dismissed on the pretext that they would be useless to him since "the constitution of Negroes . . [is] . . totally different from that of Europeans" (Ibid., p. 363).

25. Maurois, *Les Trois Dumas*, p. 25.

26. Ibid., p. 30.

27. Dumas, *père*, *My Memoirs*, trans. and ed. A. Craig Bell (Chilton Book Company Division, 1961), p. 17.

28. Dumas, *père*, *Le Comte de Monte Cristo*, 3 vols. (Livre de Poche, 1973), 3:192.

29. Dumas, *père*, *The Road to Monte Cristo: A Condensation from the Memoirs of Alexandre Dumas*, trans. James Eckert Goodman (New York: Charles Scribner's Sons, 1956), p. 202. Dumas refers to his "faintly creole" accent.

30. Arthur F. Davidson, *Alexandre Dumas: His Life and Works* (Westminster: Archibald Constable & Co., 1902), p. 201.

31. Maurois, *Les Trois Dumas*, p. 13.

32. Schopp, *Alexandre Dumas*, pp. 9–10, and Dumas, *père*, *My Memoirs*, p. 18.

33. Dumas, *père*, *My Memoirs*, p. 14.

34. Hemmings, *Alexandre Dumas*, p. 17.

35. Dumas, *père*, *The Road to Monte Cristo*, p. 3.

36. Dumas, *père*, *My Memoirs*, p. 29.

37. Hemmings, *Alexandre Dumas*, pp. 204–5.

38. Madelon Bedell, *The Alcotts: Biography of a Family*, (New York: Clarkson N. Potton, Inc., 1980), p. 149.

39. Richard Wright, *Black Boy: A Record of Childhood and Youth* (New York: Harper and Row, 1989, original 1937), p. 267–68.

40. It is fair to note, however, that it was not completely unknown, in the eighteenth and nineteenth centuries, for a white woman to give birth to a mulatto child. Lemuel B. Haynes (1753–1833), a well-known black preacher, was the son of a white woman and a slave (see *Black Writers of America: A Comprehensive Anthology*, ed. Richard Barksdale and Keneth Kinnamon, [MacMillan, 1972], p. 226). In Harriet E. Wilson's novel *Our Nig* (1859), which Henry Louis Gates, Jr., believes to be autobiographical (see *Figures in Black: Words, Signs, and the "Racial" Self* [New York and Oxford University Press, 1987], p. 126), the character Frado has a mother who is white, though she is black. Both the real man and the fictional little girl were deserted, however, by mothers who were unable to support a kind of social disapproval and ostracism that Mme. Dumas neither expected nor received. Her parents and family were flattered when Thomas-Alexandre sought her hand in marriage (he had been living in their house, billeted there by the army) and the only stipulation her father made was that the young black reach the rank of general before the wedding took place (see Maurois *Les Trois Dumas*, p. 13).

41. Well-known black expatriates to France in our century include Josephine Baker, James Baldwin, Richard Wright, and recently, Barbara Chase-Riboud.

42. Davidson, *Alexandre Dumas*, p. 45, and Maurois, *Les Trois Dumas*, p. 78.

43. Hemmings, *Alexandre Dumas*, p. 135.

44. Ibid., p. 54.

45. Maurois, *Les Trois Dumas*, p. 401.

46. Davidson, *Alexandre Dumas*, p. 45.

47. Davidson reproduces this sketch on p. 288.

48. John C. Miller, *The Wolf by the Ears: Thomas Jefferson and Slavery* (New York: MacMillan, 1977), pp. 273–74.

49. Dumas, *père*, *The Road to Monte Cristo*, p. 202, and Schopp, *Alexandre Dumas*, p. 153.

50. Maurois, *Les Trois Dumas,* p. 266, and Hemmings, *Alexandre Dumas,* p. 154.

51. Maurois, *Les Trois Dumas,* p. 266.

52. Dumas, *père, My Memoirs,* p. 207, and Schopp, *Alexandre Dumas,* p. 79.

53. Sulzberger, *Fathers and Children,* p. 53.

54. Hemmings, *Alexandre Dumas,* p. 143.

55. Ibid., p. 139.

56. Dumas, *père, My Memoirs,* p. 195.

57. Hemmings, *Alexandre Dumas,* p. 148.

58. Schopp, *Alexandre Dumas,* p. 323.

59. Ibid., p. 475.

60. The famous letter from the novel in which Armand breaks off with Marguerite, telling her, "I'm not rich enough to love you as I would like, or poor enough to be loved as you would like," is a word for word reproduction of one that Dumas *fils* wrote to Marie Duplessis on August 30, 1845 (see Maurois, *Les Trois Dumas,* p. 222). He began the novel after rereading her letters to him after her death.

61. Dumas, Alexandre, *fils, La Dame aux Caméllias* (Paris: Gallimard, 1975), p. 42.

62. Ibid., p. 349.

63. Maurois, *Les Trois Dumas,* pp. 487–89.

64. Schopp, *Alexandre Dumas,* p. 308.

65. Dumas, *père, My Memoirs,* pp. 103–4.

66. Maurois, *Les Trois Dumas,* p. 35.

67. Ibid., p. 34.

68. Dumas, *père, My Memoirs,* pp. 25–8.

69. Dumas, *père, The Road to Monte Cristo,* p. 43.

70. Lomax, Alan, and Raoul Abdul, ed., *3,000 Years of Black Poetry* (Greenwich, Conn.: Fawcett Publishing House, 1970), p. 87.

71. See Dorothy Trench-Bonett, "Alexander Pushkin – Black Russian Poet," *The Black Scholar,* 20 no. 2, March/April 1989, pp. 2–9. *The Negro of Peter the Great* can be found in Alexander Sergeyevitch Pushkin, *The Captain's Daughter and Other Great Stories,* trans. T. Keane (New York: Random House, 1936), pp. 209–310.

72. Although he translated one story by Pushkin as "La Boule de Neige," including "Le Chasse-Neige" (see Davidson's list of Dumas' works in *Alexandre Dumas*), after his trip to Russia, Dumas, who could neither speak or read Russian, used a crib for this translation. Russia was considered a barbarous, backwards, "Asiatic" country by Western

Europeans in Dumas' time; they knew nothing of Russian literature, and Dumas probably considered the Pushkin story a curiosity. I am unable to find any evidence that he knew that Pushkin was also black, nor could I figure out which of Pushkin's works was translated under that title.

73. Schopp, *Alexandre Dumas*, p. 93.

74. Ibid., p. 45.

75. Dumas, *père, Mes Mémoires*, quoted in Parigot, *Alexandre Dumas*, p. 26.

76. Maurice Valency, *The Flower and the Castle: An Introduction to Modern Drama* (New York: MacMillan, 1963), pp. 75, 76.

77. Maurois, *Les Trois Dumas*, p. 89.

78. Valency, *The Flower and the Castle*, p. 50. In 1843, Francois Ponsard's Lucrece, a drama in the classic style, had an unexpected success, and no dramas were produced in the Romantic style after this until the brief revival with Rostand.

79. The Chilton Company Book Division (Peter Owen) has translated several of these travel guides into English under the titles *Travels in Switzerland, From Paris to Cadiz, Tangier to Tunis,* and *Adventures in Czarist Russia.*

80. Hemmings, *Alexandre Dumas*, p. 126.

81. Alexandre Dumas, *père, Georges,* (New York: Random House, 1975).

82. Frances Miltoun, *Dumas' Paris* (Boston: L.C. Page & Co, 1905), p. 47.

83. Hemmings, *Alexandre Dumas*, p. 125.

84. See, for example, Alexandre Dumas, *père, Monte Cristo*, Livrede Piche, 1973, (3 volumes), vol. 3, p. 196. Interestingly, in *Monte Cristo*, there is not only the white slave, Haydee, but also a black slave, Ali. Ali has had his tongue cut out, however; he is a mute. Did Dumas make him mute, I wonder, because of the lack of success he had had until this point in trying to tell the stories of blacks?

85. Hemmings, *Alexandre Dumas*, pp. 126–27 and Maurois, *Les Trois Dumas*, pp. 246–51, both give synopses of the true story of Francois Picaud, used as a basis for *Monte Cristo*, and discuss the many changes Dumas made for his plot. Hemmings also provides an excellent critical study of Dumas' novel on pp. 127–30.

86. Hemmings, *Alexandre Dumas*, p. 137–38.

87. Maurois, *Les Trois Dumas*, pp. 205–6.

88. See ibid., pp. 202–8 for a frank discussion of Dumas, Maquet, and the question of plagiarism vs. collaboration.

89. *The Three Musketeers*

90. See foreword to Alexandre Dumas, *père, The Man in the Iron Mask.* (Dodd Mead, 1944).

91. Dumas, *père, My Memoirs*, p. 213.

92. Schopp, *Alexandre Dumas*, p. 186.

93. Maurois, *Les Trois Dumas*, p. 126.

94. Ibid., p. 117.

95. Dumas, *père, The Road to Monte Cristo*, pp.307, 317.

96. Ibid., p. 311.

97. Davidson, *Alexandre Dumas*, p. 160.

98. Hippolyte Parigot, *Le Drame d'Alexandre Dumas: Etude Dramatique, Sociale et Litteraire* (Paris: Calmann Levy, 1899), p. 212.

99. Davidson, *Alexandre Dumas*, p. 161, and Parigot, *Drame*, p. 67. This remark was made in the preface to *Le Fils Naturel* (1858).

100. *Black Writers of America*, p.41, 47.

101. Dumas, *Charles VII*, act 1, scene 2, pp. 13–14.

102. Dumas, *père, My Memoirs*, p. 213.

103. Maurois, *Les Trois Dumas*, p. 126.

104. The others were Schiller's Hassan and Scott's Hayraddin Maugrabin.

105. William Shakespeare, *Othello*, (New York: Washington Square Press, 1957), act 1, scene 3, p. 17.

106. Ibid., act 1, scene 2, p. 11.

107. *Charles VII*, act 4, scene 1, p. 44.

108. Note the debt to Racine's Andromaque. Parigot discusses Dumas' originality, though, and the changes he made in the plot he got from the classic writer's great play (*Drame*, p. 213).

109. *Charles VII*, act 1, scene 1, pp. 8, 9.

110. Ibid., act 2, scene 5, p. 28, and act 1, scene 2, pp. 12–13.

111. Ibid., pp. 13, 10, 22, 23.

112. Ibid., act 2, scene 7, p. 33.

113. Maurois, *Les Trois Dumas*, p. 126.

114. *Charles VII*, act 1, scene 1, p. 8, and act 2, scene 6, p. 31.

115. Parigot, *Drame*, pp. 198–202.

116. *Charles VII* act 4, scene 6, p. 52.

117. Ibid., act 3, scene 4, p. 41.

118. Ibid., act 2, scene 3, p. 25.

Bibliography

Bastide, Roger. *African Civilisations in the New World*. Trans. Peter Green. New York: Harper and Row, 1971.

Black Writers of America: A Comprehensive Anthology. ed. Richard Barksdale and Keneth Kinnamon. New York: Macmillan, 1972.

de Bury, Blaze. *Alexandre Dumas, Sa Vie, Son Temps, Son Oeuvre*. Paris: Ancienne Maison Michel Levy Freres, 1885.

Davidson, Arthur F. *Alexandre Dumas, His Life and Works*. Westminister: Archibald Constable & Co., 1902.

Dumas, Alexandre, *fils. La Dame aux Camellias*. Paris: Gallimard, 1975.

Dumas, Alexandre, *père. Charles VII chez ses grands vassaux, (Tragedie en cinq actes)*. Paris: Charles Lemesle, 1831.

Dumas, Alexandre, *père. Le Comte de Monte Cristo*. 3 vols. Livre de Poche, 1973.

Dumas, Alexandre, *père. My Memoirs*. Trans. A. Craig Bell. Chilton Company Book Division, 1961.

Dumas, Alexandre, *père. The Road to Monte Cristo: A Condensation from the Memoirs of Alexandre Dumas*. Ed. Jules Ekert Goodman. New York: Charles Scribner's Sons, 1956.

Dumas, Alexandre, *père. Les Trois Mousquetaires*. G.F. Flammarion, 1984.

Dumas, Alexandre, *père. La Tulipe Noire*. Collection Nelson, Calmann-Levy.

Dumas, Alexandre, *père. Vingt Ans Apres*. 2 vols. G.F. Flammarion.

Gates, Henry Louis, Jr. *Figures in Black: Words, Signs and the "Racial" Self*. New York and Oxford: Oxford University Press, 1987.

Hemmings, F. W. J. *Alexandre Dumas: The King of Romance*. New York: Charles Scribner's Sons, 1979.

James, C. L. R. *The Black Jacobins: Toussaint L'Ouverture and the San Domingo Revolution*. 2nd ed. New York: Random House, 1963.

Maurois, André. *Les Trois Dumas*. Paris: Librairie Hachette, 1957.

Maurois, André. *Three Musketeers: A Study of the Dumas Family*. Translation of *Les Trois Dumas* by Gerald Hopkins. London: Jonathan Cape, 1957.

Miltoun, Frances. *Dumas' Paris*. Boston: L.C. Page & Co., 1905.

Miquel, Pierre. *Histoire de France*. Libraire Artheme Fayard, 1976.

Parigot, Hippolyte. *Alexandre Dumas, père*. Paris: Librairie Hachette, 1902.

Parigot, Hippolyte. *Le Drame d'Alexandre Dumas: Etude Dramatique, Sociale et Litteraire*. Paris: Calmann Levy, 1899.

Robertson, J. G. "Other Sturmer und Dranger: Schiller's Early Years." *A History of German Literature*. William Blackwood & Sons, Ltd., 1949. Pp. 326–38.

Schopp, Claude. *Alexandre Dumas: Genius of Life*. Trans. A. J. Koch. New York and Toronto: Franklin Watts, 1988.

Scott, Sir Walter, *Quentin Durward*. New York: Dodd, Mead & Co., 1923.

Shakespeare, William. *The Tragedy of Othello, The Moor of Venice*. Folger Library Edition. New York: Washington Square Press, 1957.

Sulzberger, C. L. *Fathers and Children: How Famous Leaders Were Influenced by Their Fathers*. New York: Arbor House, 1987. Pp. 39–57.

Valency, Maurice. *The Flower and the Castle: An Introduction to Modern Drama*. New York: Macmillan, 1963. Pp. 11–90.

Charles VII at the
Homes of His Great Vassals

A TRAGEDY IN FIVE ACTS

CHARACTERS IN THE PLAY

CHARLES VII, King of France
CHARLES OF SAVOISY, lord of Seignelais
YACOUB, a young Arab, usually called 'the Saracen'
JOHN, BASTARD OF ORLEANS, Count of Mortain, of Dunois and
   of Longueville
GUY-RAYMOND, an archer
ANDREW and JOHN, two other archers
THE CHAPLAIN
BALTHAZAR, the falconer
BERENGARIA, Countess of Savoisy
AGNES SOREL
ISABELLE OF GRAVILLE

SCENE: The action takes place at the castle of Seignelais, in the
province of Berry, France.

TRANSLATOR'S NOTE: The year is 1422, the year of Charles VII's
ascension, during the Hundred Years War. The English have
invaded and occupied almost all of France and, in fact, since
the Treaty of Troyes (1420), Henry VI of England has been
recognized as heir to the French throne. He is a baby; his
uncle the Duke of Bedford is regent and *de facto* ruler of
England and France.

(The stage is set to represent a room in the Gothic style. To
the rear, in the center, is an arched Gothic door looking out
on a courtyard with stained glass windows in the shape of
crosses. To the right of the audience is a door concealed by a
tapestry. To the left is a large fireplace and another door, also
concealed by a tapestry, abutting the chamber of honor.
Crosses on all sides and genuine suits of armour hang between the doors. Near the fireplace is a prayer-stool.

Charles VII at the
Homes of His Great Vassals

ACT I

Scene I

[*Several archers, encircling the fireplace. On the opposite side,* YACOUB *lies on a tiger skin. A pilgrim and an archer, carrying a freshly killed stag on his shoulders, appear simultaneously in the door to the rear.*]

Pilgrim. [*On the threshold.*] God be with you all!

Andrew. [*Passing in front of him.*] Come in, Father. If our lord Charles of Savoisy were here and saw you standing on his threshold like this he would say, as I do, "Father, come in."

Pilgrim. My thanks. [*Yacoub trembles and turns around at the sound of his voice.*]

Andrew. And if he were here, he would also say, "Sit in my own seat, Father, and drink from my cup." So sit; and drink; because, by the true God! We're under orders to say it in his place. [*To the archers.*] Isn't that right?

Archers. Most certainly.

Pilgrim. And I'll presently do just that. But in order to better repay his kindness, may I go first to pray for his ancestors at their tombs; since I know that he is a pious son of the church?

Andrew. [*Unhooking a key.*] John, take this key and guide this holy man. [*Exeunt Pilgrim and John*]. Now, let one of you who's a famed hunter of deer tell me if many, fired on from one hundred twenty paces, fall as this one did, with one shot. [*He throws the stag on the ground.*] Look. [*They surround the animal.*]

An Archer. It's a stag of royal lineage!

Andrew. I discovered his tracks at daybreak. I had to go like a boar through copse and thicket to follow him; that's how I got blood on my hands and face. [*To Yacoub.*] You laugh?

An Archer. Don't pay attention to that savage.

Yacoub. [*Turning around.*] Humph!

An Archer. Does he know anything about the art of hunting? Hunting is the sport of nobles; of Christians.

Yacoub. [*Speaking as if to himself.*] I was still a child; one morning my father returned to his tent—panting, with fiery eyes. He threw down his bow and his arrows and said to me, "By Mohammed, Yacoub, this district is accursed! Each night I lose a sheep from my flock. The lioness came back to the sheepfold again; I saw her heavy prints on the sand. No doubt she has little ones in some lair." I didn't answer. But when my father left I took the bow and arrows and bent over the earth, I followed the lioness. She had crossed the Nile at the same place where I crossed it—she thought to hide her flight from me in the desert. I went into the desert, hot in pursuit of her. She had found shade at the foot of the great granite sphinx, ancient sentinel of the ancient desert, avoiding the zenith of the sun. Tired like her, I lay down like her—like her I took up my course again, and until evening my steps crowded her steps. And then I ceased to see her, and stood still praying for a single sound to come to me that I could seize on. . . . I listened, holding my breath, floating on that sea of sand. In a moment one could hear a muffled roaring in the distance—I glided towards it through the shadows, like a serpent. A lair opened its dark gullet in my path. And in its depths I, unafraid, caught sight of two glistening eyes which fixed themselves on me. I had no more need of sounds, or tracks, because we were face to face, that lioness and I. . . . Oh! that was a dreadful and daring combat. Both the man and the lioness roared, but the roars of one of them were snuffed out. And then the sand was stained with the blood of one of them, and when day came it cast its light on a child who slept next to a dead lion. That child can't be a model for Christians, though. Hunting is the sport of infidels—

Andrew. Shut up, you Saracen! When Christians go hunting in your maize fields, far from their own country, it's because they are troubled by a holy hope. . . . [*Points to Yacoub.*] And look at the game they bring back to France! [*He takes the arrows out of his belt and leans his bow in a corner.*] Ouf! I'm thirsty now. Let's drink, companions! What are they saying about the English? What are the Burgundians doing? What's new, since yesterday? [*He drinks.*] Ah! Burgundy! Burgundy, which makes war on us so shamelessly! I can quarrel with your children—but never, Burgundy, with your wine!

An Archer. New? Guy-Raymond has arrived.

Andrew. From where?

An Archer. From the French camp, I think.

Andrew. God reward him if he comes to tell us that the English are beaten, or that the king has regained even a little virtue. Did he give you any news, in passing?

An Archer. The Countess had him brought to her as soon as he arrived. When he passed by here he told us only to wait a moment for him.

Andrew. He probably brings a message from the master?

An Archer. It's probable.

Andrew. I'll watch for him with you in the passageway. It will soon be three years since he left here; he must have something new to tell.

Scene II

[Guy–Raymond *comes out of the Countess' room.*]

Raymond. [*To Andrew.*] Here I am. Greetings.

Archers. Greetings, Raymond.

Raymond. Greetings to you with your red, puffy face. Are you still a hunter? Are you still a drunk? [*Andrew shows him the stag. Andrew shows him the empty bottle.*] Bravo! I don't know anyone who neglects the gifts that God gave every man, except peasants of low birth. [*Approaching Yacoub.*] And you, young tiger?

Yacoub. Harumph!

Raymond. Hear him growl. Don't you know that if it hadn't been for me, you impure little Saracen, you would still be roaring in your accursed desert? And you wouldn't have that gold collar around your neck which gives you rank among the footmen, that anyone but a dog can look upon and read: "Yacoub, the Saracen, property of Sir Charles of Savoisy, lord of Seignelais." I took you, naked as a reptile, out of the sun. You owe bread, clothes and shelter to me, you slave; and if you've forgotten that, I have returned to make you remember.

Yacoub. Fine. I remember.

Andrew. Well, come here, Raymond, and tell us something about the affairs of the times.

Raymond. I suppose you all know that Charles VI is dead and that the young king had himself quickly crowned at Poitiers.[1]

Andrew. By my faith! We know nothing, buried here in the depths of this fortress! Even though, by God, all of this concerns us—we're Armagnacs[2] and Frenchmen. We wear the white cross on our clothes.

Raymond. It seems, my sheep, that your flock goes without knowing who's leading it. You're men of Berry, and they're fighting in Maine, yet you know nothing of it. Well, I believe that, without leaving this place, those of you who are curious could soon hear and see some marvels from the tops of these battlements if they opened their eyes and listened with their ears!

---

[1] The King of France could only be crowned at Reims, which was then in the hands of the English. The coronation of the historical Charles VII at Poitiers in 1422 was temporary, not really valid. He was officially still "the Dauphin" (French equivalent of "Prince of Wales") until Joan of Arc's victories made his real coronation possible on July 17, 1429.

[2] The ARMAGNACS and the BURGUNDIANS were the two factions in the civil war that split France in the early fifteenth century, allowing Henry V of England to conquer it more easily.

An Archer. Well—what would they see? What would they hear?

Raymond. They would see thirty thousand soldiers (Satan choke them!) coming like a wall of iron from the front, some shouting "Burgundy!" and the others "Saint George!"[3]

Andrew. What! The English and Burgundians so near us? Thirty thousand, you say?

Raymond. Exactly that, comrades. And they say that a great crowd is coming from Brittany to aid them in the battle.

An Archer. From three sides, then. . . . But Paris?

Raymond. Surrendered.

Andrew. And Count Bernard, who held it?

Raymond. Hung. Henry VI of England is named King of France; Bedford regent.

An Archer. Hell!

Raymond. But Clarence, Suffolk and Lord Grey, fortunately killed before Angers, prove to our soldiers that foreign hearts are not out of the reach of a French lance— well hidden though they are behind English armor. Bedford has just signed a treaty with Philip and John, though. If it goes into effect—if the Duke of Burgundy and the Duke of Brittany join forces with the English to make war—by the true God, there'll be nothing left for us to do but beg for mercy. Unless Charles VII—if only he could be here to

---

[3] SAINT GEORGE was the patron saint of England, and the English used "Saint George for Merry England" as their battle cry. The Duke of Burgundy had allied himself with the English while the Armagnacs supported Charles VII.

listen to the wish of my heart! — unless, unfurling the *oriflamme*[4] with his royal hand the king charges at the head of the barons united by his voice, shouting aloud: "Mountjoy and St. Dennis!"[5] For cursed is he who, deaf to that valiant cry, can hear it without raising sword or lance!

Andrew. I know someone, though, who will wait very calmly for the moment to be either English or French.

Raymond. Who?

Andrew. [*Pointing to Yacoub.*] Him.

Raymond. [*Speaking to Yacoub.*] Is it true?

Yacoub. It's true. What do they matter to me, in my hovel — Armagnac of the white cross or Burgundy of the red cross? What does it matter to me which is the weak one or the powerful one? Neither Charles or Henry has rights over my blood. There will come a day when either France or England must save six feet of earth for Yacoub the son of Asshan — and whatever their hearts' desires while they're alive, neither Charles or Henry will get more than that when dead.

Raymond. Take care, though, that the executioner doesn't lead you to take possession of your last domain, and doesn't string your bones up halfway to the sky, like the tomb that

---

[4] The ORIFLAMME was the banner of the French kings from the twelfth to the fifteenth centuries. Square and red, it was flown in battle as a flag would be today.

[5] "MOUNTJOIE ET SAINT DENIS!" was the battle cry of France. St. Dennis is, of course, the patron saint of Paris.

Ishmael worships![6] Perhaps someday God may permit that.

Andrew. And when did you leave the Count, our master?

Raymond. It will soon be a month since we both left the camp at Beaugé. He went towards Brittany and I took the opposite road. I had a commission to perform that wasn't easy. I had to open a passage for myself to Avignon by ruse or iron, get past the English and Burgundians and give an important message to the Holy Father.[7] I did it—here I am! By my faith, it won't be a bad thing if the Count, on his part, manages as I did. I hope I brought the letter back in good order. Look—there's Benedict's seal, very clear, with the keys, the crosier, the cross and papal tiara. Cross yourselves.

[*All make the sign of the cross. Raymond signals Yacoub to do as much. Yacoub folds his arms across his breast and bows his head.*]

Yacoub. Let it be done the way you do it. Jesus and Mohammed are two powerful prophets.

Raymond. [*To Yacoub, pulling out his dagger.*] Look at this dagger. Yacoub, if it ever comes to pass that you mix up two names, I swear this iron will nail your tongue to your palate, stopping your harangue at the first word!

---

[6] " . . . the tomb that Ishmael worships . . . " Ishmael, Abraham's illegitimate son by Hagar, was the ancestor of the Arabs according to both the Bible and the Koran. "Ishmael" worships Mohammed.

[7] The Pope referred to is Benedict XIII (c. 1324–1423), actually an "antipope" during the period when there were two popes, one at Avignon in France and the other at Rome, in the Vatican. He had refused to abdicate in 1417. His authority, therefore, is dubious.

All. [*Coming towards him.*] Death to the blasphemer!

Yacoub. [*Standing and putting his hand on his scimitar.*] Don't come near me, cursed ones! Get back. . . . by Allah! Get back, I tell you. . . .

Scene III

[*Enter* BERENGARIA, *Countess of Savoisy, raising the tapestry. Everyone stops when they see her. Yacoub folds his arms across his breast and remains in an attitude of the most profound respect.*]

Beren. Come, children—still all this noise! A quarrel? Who are you bullying like this?

Andrew. It's the infidel who's blaspheming.

Beren. Eh! Does he know what he's saying, you madmen? Isn't it enough that God rejects him? Raymond; what were you doing with that dagger?

Raymond. Nothing, madam. . . . [*Throwing it at Yacoub's feet.*] I ordered Yacoub to sharpen the blade. . . . Do you understand, Saracen?

Beren. That's enough. Leave, all of you. Come back this evening to pray with us. [*They leave.*] Yacoub, we're alone now. Tell me, what was it this time?

Yacoub. Nothing.

Beren. What did they do to you?

Yacoub. Nothing.

Beren. See—I don't know what just happened and yet I'm saying that they're wrong and you're right.

Yacoub. Thanks.

Beren. Well; don't you have anything else to say to me?

Yacoub. Indeed. Mohammed has the right to curse, and he curses.

Beren. Yacoub!

Yacoub. I don't know why. . . . I only know that I am cursed; that my hatred becomes deeper each day; and that my mother died bringing me into the world.

Beren. Unhappy man!

Yacoub. Unhappy? Unhappy, indeed. For, tell me, what have I done that I should suffer like this? Is it my fault that your husband and master followed a vassal into a church, and there, in spite of the cries of the priest, struck him a mortal blow—that the blood spurted on the altar? Is it my fault that in his stupid rage he forgot that a church is a place of asylum? Is it my fault? And if, by the university, the angry Holy Father said that, in penance for this sin, the count had to arm a galley to appease the anger of heaven, and bringing desolation to our shores had to make us slaves in expiation—is that my fault? And can't I complain that *his* crime came to overtake *me*, deep in my desert? Oh—if some tribal chieftain on the shores of the Nile came into the bosom of your family, woman, where everything was thriving, and took your son or father from you for such a crime, with such an aim; if they treated him over there the way that I'm treated here; if they put a collar like this around his neck—you would understand that hatred doesn't go back into the soul as easily as this blade into this sheath!

Beren. Yes. You really are unhappy.

Yacoub. [*Melancholy.*] What child was more happy than I was, more triumphant than me? When my burning head weighs down on my hands heavily and my slow memory retraces its path in the past, going from landmark to landmark, like a man forced to walk backwards, I dream of my morning; so beautiful that it seems like a lie to me and I forget the present and future. I no longer have a collar; I no longer have a prison; I feel a warm sun in a boundless horizon; I see the long caravan unroll itself like a marbled serpent on the hot savannah, the places for meals chosen in advance. I know where the desert hides its oases. . . . Go on, courage, go on, my Arab camel drivers! repeat for me your magic–syllabled songs. Invoke Mohammed, the torch of the East, a camel driver like you, fighting and praying; going like you from Mecca to Medina. . . . Or don't you know the grenadine song that black–eyed Almée sings before our tent in the evening, by the Nile's shore, turning around and around until the happy moment when her gauze tunic clings to her lovely body, doubling our ecstacy; and my father makes a mask of gold for her, with sequins,[8] spreading a treasure on her damp forehead. For my father is not a common chief, at Saïd. He has four arrows of war in his quiver and when he bends his bow and hurls them as a signal to his four tribes, towards four targets, each takes the time an eagle takes to stretch his wings and sends him a hundred faithful horsemen. [*Falling down dejected*] Oh, Mohammed, have mercy! It's an overwhelming dream. A dream of Paradise, but with a bloody awakening. And I come out of this dream into a night of tears, a dagger in my breast, captive of an armed man who came across me while I slept. The man

---

[8] SEQUINS, in this context, refers to a kind of gold coin.

is Raymond. The iron. . . . [*Picking up the dagger that Raymond threw to him.*] it's this dagger. When I saw him again I felt my ten years of slavery roar around me like a storm. Your dagger—your dagger—Yes, I'll sharpen it just as you wish. Then I'll return it to you.

Beren. Yet they told me that your wound was quick to heal, Yacoub, thanks to the care of the Count.

Yacoub. Yes; I know that the Count was kind to me. He stretched out his hand to the dying slave. He poured on my lip, in that last hour, all the rest of the water he was saving for himself—water, so scarce in the desert at that moment that each drop was as costly as a diamond! That's what makes the scales tip in his favor, that's what my heart weighs in silence when Hell comes to tempt me during my long nights to return tears for tears, blow for blow, iron for iron.

Beren. But since the time he took you from your shore, can you really call your state slavery? Aren't you free in the mornings, after day has dawned?

Yacoub. Yes—but except for him everyone has insults in their mouths when they speak to me. I strike myself and tear at everything I touch. And if for me he softens the law of slavery, does his country soften itself for me, as he does? I am not at my ease between these thick walls. The air which suffices for you weighs on my chest. My eyes wear themselves out piercing your narrow horizon; your sun is pale and your day short. Oh! rather the *simoun*![9] Yes, even if its flaming sea buries me alive under its hot blade!

---

[9] The SIMOUN is a hot and violent desert wind.

Beren. Yet I've seen joyous flashes succeed sad looks in your eyes while I've spoken to you.

Yacoub. Yes—that's the strange effect that the sight of an angel has on mortal glances. Oh! when you speak to me—when your conqueror's accent goes to seek each sleeping fiber in my heart—it seems as if my soul, stolen from this world, waits for a new life from your breath, and that happiness would be to live at your knees, angel. . . .

Beren. And if the angel were more unhappy than you, Yacoub? And if my oppressed soul and mind nourished more sinister thoughts than yours. . . . You complain of your fate. What would you say of mine?

Yacoub. That I'm really accursed, because I can do nothing to console you—you, who console others—except if it were to forget my griefs for yours. Listen, though—if by chance there were some man whom it hurt you to look at—if his days had such an influence on your days that only his death could end your suffering—even if he had received the right to hurt you from Mohammed—it would only be necessary to point him out to me when he passed. And from that time on I would become a shadow for his shadow. And even if the sun were hot, or the night dark; whatever road he took to escape me, I would find the place and means to strike. And no flight could protect his head from the iron—even if he mounted the prophet's horse Al-Borack!

Beren. Yacoub, what are you saying?

Yacoub. I forgot—forgive me—that you already have a protector here.

Beren. But who?

Yacoub. The Count.

Beren. [*Alarmed.*] And no one comes to tell me, "Berengaria, your husband is here."

Yacoub. He wants to hide his return from us, because of cares that are unknown to me as they are to you. He came knocking on doors he could have opened to him as a master, barefoot, in the robe of a priest, with a rope around his waist.

Beren. Are you very sure? Who pointed him out to you?

Yacoub. I just recognized him.

Beren. How?

Yacoub. He spoke. For the Arab lost on the faraway strand, there is no uncertain clamor in the desert; and all his stretched senses hear nature speaking at once with all its voices. He knows, no matter what distance each little sound comes from, whether it's the sound of water flowing on the bank; the murmuring of wind in the leaves of the *nopal*; the speech of men; the jackals' cries—and each of these sounds, so light that they only graze him, engrave themselves on his memory where they remain for always. How then could I mistake that voice whose sound has made me tremble so many times?

Beren. That's it! I understand. . . . The count no doubt gave a rendezvous to Raymond—what shame for me!—and returns in disguise—It's to get the letter from the Holy Father before seeing me— I understand. Everything now is clear to me because— alas!—I foresaw this shame only too well. Yacoub, I said it to you in my fright—I am the more unhappy of us two.

Yacoub. I don't understand. Go on. . . .

Beren. Be silent! Here's the chaplain coming to pray. Oh, whatever the God whose laws you follow, pray to Him for me, Yacoub. Pray!

Scene IV

[*Enter the* CHAPLAIN, RAYMOND, ANDREW, *all the archers, the valets or squires.*]

Chaplain. [*Puts a Bible on the prayer stool and turns, saying*] Are you all here, my children?

Beren. Yes, Father.

Chaplain. Have you prayed to God for the souls that the fires of hell consume in their flames; and that He should, above all, be merciful to those whose bodies rest in this place?

Beren. Yes, father.

Chaplain. Have you prayed to God to permit that a son should at last be born to the Count, our master, for fear that if death struck him today his ancient house would perish with him?

Beren. Yes, father.

Chaplain. It is well. From Him who consoles, hear now the Divine Word. Genesis, chapter sixteen:[10] "Now Sarai,

---

[10] GENESIS, CHAPTER SIXTEEN. Dumas made an error here and had the Chaplain say that he was reading from chapter six. Verses 1,2,3,4, and 15 are read. Dumas changed the biblical text to read "son" where it actually says "child."

Abram's wife bore him no children and she had an hand-maid, an Egyptian, whose name was Hagar; And Sarai said unto Abram, 'Behold now, the Lord hath restrained me from bearing. . . . ' "

Beren. Father, appease the angry Lord, who has cursed me also in my sterility.

Chaplain. [*Continuing.*] "And he went in unto Hagar and she conceived. And Hagar bore Abram a son and Abram called his son's name, whom Hagar bore, Ishmael." Kneel children, so that I may bless you now.

Raymond. [*Going to Yacoub, who is sharpening the point of the dagger.*] Wait, father, one of us pretends he doesn't understand you—[*To Yacoub.*] Kneel! Do you hear me, Saracen? I'm speaking to you—kneel!

Yacoub. [*Looking at him.*] Archer, I've heard that King Charles sometimes gives an order to the noble barons who pass in front of him, and that they obey; that these barons have the right to express in their turn their supreme desires to the squire who makes a vow to serve them and that the squire hurries to obey. Then, passing on the orders that he's given, the squire says to the archer, "Do what I say." But who ever said that the archer, who is nothing, dares give an order to anyone but his dog?

Raymond. Let the example you cite serve as your model. Obey the archer, infidel Saracen—because who says Saracen says "dog."

Yacoub. By hell! [*Strikes him with the dagger he sharpened.*] This one at least bites with steel teeth!

Raymond. [*Falling.*] Ah! Malediction!

All the Archers. [*Approaching.*] Raymond! Raymond!

Yacoub. [*Making a circle with his scimitar.*] Get back! Know that his death belongs entirely to me, and that any one of you who tries to steal a drop of his blood from me will pay with his own blood. Let none advance, therefore, or—by the Prophet!—I'll make his head fly like a child's rattle!

[*He puts one knee on the ground, to get nearer to Raymond, who is floundering.*]

Ah! Raymond. Look how in my turn I have you panting at my feet, just as I did at yours. Only no one comes to your deathbed to quench the thirst in your mouth with some drops of water. . . . But if thirst presses you, archer, put your mouth on your wound and drink your own blood.—Fix your gaze on mine, don't avoid my eyes— Your agony's too quick. —Archer, you die too fast!

Raymond. [*Holding out Benedict's letter.*] Ah! For the Count . . . [*He dies.*]

Yacoub. [*Kicking the corpse.*] Slave and serf to the end. Take him now. The lion is hungry no longer.

Scene V

[CHARLES OF SAVOISY *appears at the door, with attendants and guards.*]

Charles. What's this noise? What does this mean, masters? By the three golden chevrons, arms of my ancestors! Have you forgotten, you who are shouting in this way, that no one speaks loudly when the master is here?

[*He throws off his pilgrim's habit and appears in complete armor.*]

What's this letter? [*He picks up the Pope's letter.*] And what's
that man doing there? Raymond, my archer—dead! Just
as surely as I am called Charles of Savoisy, lord of Seignelais, his killers will die at my hand. Name them! Shut
the door, archers, so that no one escapes.

Yacoub. Master, it's I who killed him. Here I am. Strike.

Charles. [*Half drawing his sword.*] Repeat what you just said
and you will die!

Yacoub. Ten years have passed since he brought me wounded
to your arms. . . . [*Uncovering his breast.*] Here's the scar
of the blow. [*He uncovers Raymond's breast and shows the two
wounds to him.*] Master, have I struck exactly at the same
place? See! But my arm was more expert than his and the
iron entered deeper into his heart.

Charles. This is another thing, then. Since my lenience doesn't
confuse a murder with vengeance, this iron will enter its
sheath without being soiled, and I won't take the executioner's tithe. We wouldn't have believed, though that
Our first business upon arriving here would be to dis-
pense justice. But no matter. We are a Count, and a lord
of high rank, and We'll pass judgment Ourself, by God!
Children, take away the corpse and let him have a Christian tomb in consecrated ground. Farewell, my servant—
or rather, my friend—sleeping the sleep of death before
your time. Both of us were born in the same year, and I
had hoped that God would strike us both down, on the
same day, in a soldier's death, facing the English in hard
combat. We deserved that last pleasure from Him but He
judges otherwise. His will be done! [*He wipes his eyes.*]
Page, take a horse with great haste and go to Bourges
where our lord the King holds his court; and say that I will
go tomorrow to bring him my homage and that I will have

an answer to his message. [*To two archers.*] You—guard the murderer. [*To the Chaplain, ignoring Berengaria who holds out her arms.*] You, Father, come.

Beren. Not a word! [*To Yacoub.*] We are both condemned!

ACT II

Scene I

[BERENGARIA; *a page enters.*]

Beren. Well, does the Chaplain know that I request his presence at once?

Page. He's going to come, Madam.

Beren. Was he with the Count?

Page. He was leaving him.

Beren. Good. Leave me now. I don't need anything. [*The page leaves.*] I don't need anything, dear God, but mercy! Why do You grant good things to some, with Your power, while others, overwhelmed at Your feet, vainly beg Your clemency? Do You know, God, do You know what the hours of agony are like when the soul who believed in You for so so long denies You; when unhappiness pursues us step by step and we call on God, but God doesn't answer and our weak voices lose themselves, like passing breaths, without awakening an echo in space; and the soul, when no ray of hope has shined on it, is ready to appeal to Satan, he who *does* answer?

Scene II

[*The* CHAPLAIN; BERENGARIA]

Beren. Here he is. His forehead is even more severe than usual. . . . What shall I tell him?. . . . Father, reassure your child. It's the first time that the Count has returned home after three months' absence without a single word of reassuring love to soothe the wound in my heart. You —you whose help I have often begged for—you know that my heart still bleeds and groans so much in its forethought that a fear breaks it! It trembles so much, afraid that the Count will finally despise the wife who hasn't, up until now, rewarded him except with a barren marriage and a sterile love!

Chaplain. [*Drawing near her.*] He who takes the things of this world for his goal and who believes he can strengthen his solitary walk leaning on a staff from the trees that he breaks along the way, risks breaking and tearing his hand. The Supreme Master asks man to go farther, and higher; and this world itself, where the mortal traveler stumbles for a moment, is only an arch of the bridge that leads to heaven.

Beren. Father, I am only a weak woman. Speak to me in a way that will reassure my soul; don't frighten me.

Chaplain. And if, my child, I can't speak to you except in this way? Say like me, then: "Happy those families from which the hand of the Lord chooses those chaste girls who, far from a vain world, with fervent hearts, wear out the thresholds of their convents with their knees!

Beren. But God makes only virgins and widows submit to those holy trials. I'm married—to the Count.

Chaplain. My daughter, in this place you have no longer any husband but God.

Beren. Father — God Himself bound us together in front of the church —

Chaplain. [*Showing her the letter that Raymond brought back.*] And this breaks those bonds.

Beren. [*Reading.*] A decree of divorce! Oh, I suspected that the Count would come to this final means! But can a man — (for, in the end, the Holy Father is a man) — does he have the right to break those bonds because he writes from Avignon or Rome?

Chaplain. You forget that God said to this man: "Tie and untie." Daughter, the hand of God humbles you. Be like the reed which bends under His breath, not like the oak rising up to heaven which resists, breaks and only gives the more witness that the anger of God has passed over its head, by the crash spread far over the earth.

Beren. And if I resign myself to my new fate, when must I leave this place?

Chaplain. Tomorrow morning.

Beren. Will I be able to see my master for a last farewell?

Chaplain. Daughter, such a farewell would perhaps reattach your worldly soul to things down here again and the Count . . .

Beren. Alright. The Count doesn't wish it.

Chaplain. Daughter, I'm only his humble interpreter.

Beren. What else does he require?

Chaplain. Daughter, retreat is necessary for the heart that wishes to prepare itself.

Beren. I'm going to seclude myself in my apartment, Father isn't that it? I begin to understand, don't I, with the first word.

Chaplain. The Count must pass judgment here.

Beren. What judgment?

Chaplain. Against the miscreant.

Beren. Ah, yes! Yacoub—the other victim. When He created both of us, one near the Nile, the other near the Loire, do you believe, Father—myself, I can't believe it—that God read in advance that in the far-off future we would both be included in the same destiny? That the same man, becoming our master one day, would break the happiness that God wanted to place in us, and save shame for me and death for him, without us being able to avoid this fate?

Chaplain. I believe it.

Beren. And if God in His heavenly goodness had wanted to change this disastrous future into a happy destiny, did He have this power?

Chaplain. The Lord could do it, and had only to wish it.

Beren. Happy the infidel, then! And I envy him. . . . he's not a Christian, he can curse life!

Chaplain. Daughter!

Beren. Listen to me, Father, and in your turn answer me. Do you remember the day when my mother, giving me to her husband, bathed in tears of love, said to him: "A daughter is born to you?"

Chaplain. Of course. And that day was a triumphant day.

Beren. Do you also remember, Father, how the child grew under your gaze and became a woman? You read her like an open book. You could follow, with your eyes, at all moments, her hopes, her wishes, her vows, her feelings. Well; the young girl, did she have a single thought that wasn't for her mother, in her light heart? Speak.

Chaplain. Not one.

Beren. And since the time when my hand was pledged to the Count, and after the marriage when you came near to us as if in your own family so that the father could still watch over his daughter. . . . Whether the Count was here in this castle or whether you prayed for my absent husband; if I had tears in my eyes or was smiling; if my soul was sad or joyous — Say if in that soul — for you know — if ever a single thought was not for the husband. Say it aloud.

Chaplain. Not a single one. I can attest it.

Beren. And if he hadn't been taken with this fatal wish to break our bonds, and if a constant love had responded to mine until my last day — do you think that the jealous demands of God would have dared to ask of the daughter, the wife, more than she performed; and that I could have responded to Him tranquilly at the day of judgment?

Chaplain. That's my deep and sincere conviction. Why do you ask it?

Beren. I needed to hear your conviction so that, should strength abandon me in my affliction, and should I fall into some sin, that sin at least would be light on my tomb.

Chaplain. What are you saying?

Beren. I'm saying that I can't know what thoughts come to the heart when it loses all hope. . . . That the devil watches over us vigilantly and that I have, by your own confession, twenty-five years of virtue to put at God's feet as a counterweight in the scales, against a moment of forgetfulness. [*She leaves.*]

Scene III

[*The* CHAPLAIN; *then the* COUNT.]

Chaplain. Go, poor creature, and may God pardon you. Because you speak truly—you were always pious and good; and never did a child's heart shine from blue eyes, with a ray more celestial and pure!

Count. [*Enters.*] Sir. . . .

Chaplain. It's the Count!

Count. Well, you saw her. And what did she say during the interview? Poor Berengaria. Did she cry a good deal?

Chaplain. Her heart was better prepared than I would have thought. She had probably resigned herself in advance, since for some time you've scorned her. . . .

Count. Scorned her! Sir, take that back. If her love had been fertile and given me the hope of a son who would bear the name of my ancestors; or if this unfortunate country, France, weren't tottering in its unhappiness so that it

needs all its noblemen to serve as props around it to the
point that when one of them feels his arm grow tired, if
his son isn't there to take his place, the one who withdraws is anxious as he sees the throne suddenly lean towards his side; if it weren't for that I could have seen my
name become obliterated and my lineage extinguished,
rather than hurt her with one word. . . . But when
France has sunk so low as to be near its end; when the ancient monarchy rolls in its blood, falling under the blows
of threefold anarchy. . . . it's necessary, when her cries
ask them of us, to give her children. Because men pass on,
and just as if Death finds, in his domain, iron too slow to
cull his human harvest, here is Salisbury, in our dispute,
throwing artillery into the midst of combat! What will
strength and valor be worth now? Who will bear the
sword, or lift the lance, if bullets from a distance level bat-
talions like ripe ears of corn on the edges of furrows?
We're born in unprosperous times. Our fathers were
worth less than their fathers, but they were still loyal and
warlike. And here we are—worth less than they. The
panting tocsin's sound encircles our cities; there's nothing
but murder and civil war; and when the soldier finishes
and sheaths his sword, it's the executioner's turn. Well,
the hour has sounded—open the door to all—

Chaplain. To all, my lord?

Count. Yes. Sir, it's important that each man, whoever he is,
be able to enter freely near to us during the trial, because
it's necessary that each should award himself the right to
be like God in his turn, and judge the judge.

Scene IV

[*The same.* YACOUB, *between two archers; all the household of the Count.*]

Page. [*Entering.*] My lord—

Count. Silence! [*Recognizing the page that he sent to Bourges.*] Oh, Godfrey—it's you. Later you'll tell me. . . .

Page. My lord, it's the king. Our lord the king, Charles VII is following me in great haste, coming to see you in person.

Count. Our lord—at my home! . . . Hurry . . . ! No; let everyone stay in his place. It's good for the King to see how one passes judgment well sometimes, so that he can punish justly in his turn. [*To the page.*] Let King Charles VII be shown in here, just as another would be, without pomp or noise. [*The page leaves.*] Along with my consecrated ministry, God confides to me a power above the powers of the earth. And if he comes to my home while I'm passing judgment, the king's only my guest; and I'm king.

Scene V

[*The preceding; the* KING; AGNES;[11] *the King's attendants. The King entrusts the falcon he held on his wrist to a falconer. He remains standing during the trial, with Agnes, surrounded by his attendants.*]

Count. Listen now, so that everyone knows why the executioner's block and axe are in the courtyard, and why those men there are gathered around that one. Yesterday, in the same room we are in now, there was a man lying in front of these same men, crying for mercy, a dagger in his

---

[11] The historical AGNES SOREL was born around 1422, and would have been a baby at the time of the play's action. She was later the mistress of Charles VII, over whom she had great influence. She died in 1450, at about the age of twenty-eight.

heart. The one who struck him was not his conqueror—
but his killer! I wanted to know who it was, but no matter
how loudly the master questioned, no one answered him,
and the only one who spoke said to me, pointing at himself, "Here I am." Did he tell the truth? Speak.

Archers. [*Together.*] Yes, it's he! It's the slave! He killed
Raymond—Yes, Raymond, the best of us!

Count. Silence!

Archers. Then he threatened us!

Yacoub. [*Turning.*] Your master told you to be silent! Obey!

[*Everyone is silent.*]

Count. What brought the sudden scuffle on?

Yacoub. Scuffle? Not that, master; it was hatred. Do you know
what hatred is? It's hell. It's someone grinding at your
heart with iron teeth; it's a voice saying ceaselessly in
your ear: "You sleep! Awake, because your enemy keeps
watch. He'll strike tomorrow, so you had better strike today. He's coming from this side—go in front of him."
Master, when a little human blood spreads on the tiles,
staining these feudal stones, a servant comes hurriedly
behind the murderer to blot up the blood as soon as it's
shed. It isn't like that in our hot land. From the time when
one strikes with a rash hand and the blood flows, and the
sand drinks it and is deeply steeped in its color, years can
pass and the indelible stain will stay forever imprinted on
the sand. Well, in the desert there is, hidden from all
eyes, a place that has been stained with my blood for ten
years. Master, it's been ten years now since the sight of
Raymond made vengeance restless in my disturbed soul
. . . I have not shared his bread or salt at all, so that I

could keep him as my enemy, because if, forgetful, I had done the opposite, my law would have given him to me as my brother from that moment on – and I did not want that!

Count. Well; if I have pity on you, pagan, and am merciful, forgetting to ask for blood in exchange for blood and forgiving your crime because of the customs of your people – will I be able to believe that your heart will be satisfied with one murder, and won't be tempted anymore with the wish to kill? That Raymond would shut up your hatred in his tomb and that you would stay tranquilly in your chains?

Yacoub. Master, that would be a risky hope, for just one man is dead, and I hated two of them.

Count. And who is the second? For I wish to know who he is, in order to warn. . . .

Yacoub. You are the second, Master.

Count. Oh! By my patron saint! Look what memories remain in your heart after ten years of kindness! What could have been bitter during your captivity? Was France a bad mother to you? No – your fate became the same as the fate of her sons and no one took your portion either of shadow or of sun.

Yacoub. Listen. When the fertile power of Allah made two parts of the world for his children in former days, he said, smiling, to the Arabs whom he loves: "You are my elder ones, and here is the East – the land from Tangiers to Golconda is yours. And you will call this the paradise of the world." Then, with a wrathful eye, he looked afterwards at your fathers and said to them: "You will have the West."

Count. If I understand you, then, the one who stole you from your country can expect the fate of Raymond?

Yacoub. [*With deep feeling.*] Master, do you remember when I lay stretched on the sand at your feet, covered with blood? I kept asking for water and you could have taken no notice. You gave me the little that remained in your leather bottle. I remember good as well as evil and that's the reason why you aren't lying there in your turn.

Count. And if I said to you, "I break the bonds of your slavery. I was wrong to steal you, Yacoub, from your shore. From this day on, you can turn your steps towards the Nile. Here's gold. Go."

Yacoub. I wouldn't go.

Count. Who holds you in this place that I hear you curse?

Yacoub. That's my secret, Master. I can't tell it to you. Therefore, since I must neither stay or go and you may repent it whether I stay or go, believe me; pass the sentence that I deserve right now, and then tell the executioner to perform it quickly. These are my last wishes, if I can make them.

Count. [*Standing.*] Well, then, let it be done as you wish.

Yacoub. My thanks! Allah in his power, breathing on my soul in the day of my birth, made matter animate and in his goodness said, "Child, receive life with freedom." You soon stole my freedom. And now you are recapturing my life from me. . . . Thanks, master, thanks! You do as much for me with your hatred as Allah with his love.

Count. How much time do you wish to make your last farewell to the light?

Yacoub. The blink of an eye. Why should block and axe wait when body and head are ready?

Count. By Saint Charles! I'd rather see you die in your own faith than with this thoughtlessness.

Yacoub. My faith? Do I have one? And who can show me which God I should believe in, so that I can call on him? You made me renounce the God of my race, without yours taking his place in my spirit. What does my reason care for Jesus or Mohammed? No one really has the happiness that each of them promises; and in the isolation of my withered youth, thanks to you, I have no god, as I have no country.

Count. Slave, if you die with such feelings, what can you hope for?

Yacoub. To return a body to the elements—the common mass to which man in expiring brings back all that nature took away in creating him. If earth, water, air and fire formed me in the hands of chance, or of God, the wind, spreading my dust in its course will know how to return each thing to its source.

Count. What do you ask for in the hour of death?

Yacoub. Nothing; except that the executioner's axe cut well.

Count. [*To the Chaplain.*] Sir, do your duty now. Here is the Holy Book. Each time my ancestors passed an important sentence, they ordered that it be recorded in the margins that same instant, because they had the right in their castles to being justice to both high and low, and they made no mistakes. We wish to record Our judgment in the same place, and We will do as they did since We have the same right. Write, therefore [*He dictates.*] "On this day, the 20th

of the month of August, King Charles VII being present,
we have passed sentence of death on Yacoub ben Asshan,
without fear or remorse, and given up his body to the executioner, whose arms claim him. May God forgive his
soul!" Give it to me—[*He signs.*] And now take him away.

Charles VII. [*Going to the place the Count just occupied.*] Stop!
Chaplain, add this sentence underneath—that, using also
a right that his race has had for all time, King Charles VII
pardons the condemned man. [*The Count makes a movement of surprise.*] You rebel, do you wish to dispute with
me?

Count. [*Bowing.*] No. No, sire.

Agnes. [*Leaning on his shoulder.*] My lord, you are great and
good.

Count. But sire, think well. . . .

King. Yes, I understand, my host. Our right undermines high
justice. It's annoying, isn't it? Go on, pardon me for it. I
have the desire to act as king so rarely. It's my day,
today—But since the slave has troubled your house up
until this time, Count, I have a way to fix everything—
Give him to me. My jester begins to bore me. You can take
some blood horse or some trained falcon. . . . Yacoub,
do you agree to this arrangement?

Yacoub. [*Taking a dagger from one of the trophies that are near him
and raising his arm to strike himself.*] Yes—but you pay a
high price for a corpse!

All: [*Frightened.*] Ah!

Beren. [*Lifting the door-curtain without being seen.*] Live! [*She lets
the tapestry fall.*]

Count. Archers, take that dagger away from him.

Yacoub. I yield it freely. Master, fear nothing more . . . [*To himself.*] She told me to live.

King. Gentlemen, remember that that man belongs to me. [*Making a sign with his hand.*] Go—God keep you all.

Agnes. And keep the king! [*Two women approach her to take her to her apartment.*]

King. [*Going to her.*] You leave me, Agnes?

Agnes. Yes, my lord. If I remember well, the Count must give the king an account of a journey made for lofty concerns. My king doesn't want to make his Agnes take a place in this grave council—and he'll have mercy twice in the same day.

King. Yes, I understand; Agnes gives in to her fear and like a traitor in her turn, abandons her king. [*He leads her up to the door of the apartment.*]

Scene VI

[*The* KING; *the* COUNT.]

King. [*Turning towards the Count.*] Just the two of us, alone at last. Count of Savoisy, it's sheer treason to have built your manor so high that it must be sought, like an eagle's nest, at the pinnacle of a crag, so that your king, if by chance he wishes to visit an old, beloved friend, must clamber up to this place on foot, risking losing his soul twenty times as he makes oaths to God. And I tell you this without adding, my master, that if you should betray us like John VI, your walls are so high and so strong that I think they would give the king's men work for a long time.

Count. Our lord is right; but this citadel, strong as it is, is even
more faithful.

King. [*Sadly.*] My dear Count, how many have spoken to me
as you do, who have since forsworn their faith! A man's
word becomes a light thing when civil and foreign war,
pushing a state towards its destruction, fling a promise to
each ambition. [*He sits down.*]

Count. Sire, this ancient castle, since the time of its first
masters, numbers twelve of my ancestors in its burial
vaults, who sleep on their tombs in iron winding sheets
in the glimmering of funeral torches. Let's go down and
let's look for the wound on each one, where the fatal blow
pierced his armor. And afterwards the dates of their
deaths will tell us the various combats that each of them
died in. Then you will know that each of mine died for
someone of your race, struck from the front. And if you
still suspect me after this, sire, me the last of all — bad luck
to you! My father died for yours at Agincourt, and I hope
that I will die defending your rights; and later, my son, if
I have one, will die in his turn for your son, doing as I
have done.

King. Count of Savoisy, look in Our face! We are, like you, the
last of a race. Our two elder brothers, the hopes of Our
house, died — some say by poison. Phillip of Burgundy
and John VI of Brittany, my two brothers-in-law, are both
campaigning against me, and my mother, who ought to
be a strong prop for me, would buy my blood for half
hers. Each day some great vassal who abandons me falls
like a living jewel from my crown. Well! Did We hesitate
for an instant to entrust Our days to your loyalty? It's true
that Our attendants are formidable and could defend us
if the case demanded it — a woman, two pages, a jester,
three falconers. If, even at this moment, Charles of

Savoisy is weaving some plot with his disloyal hand, trying to put my royal person to death, he certainly has a murderous combat to fear—with me dressed in velvet while he's covered with steel! [*leaning on his shoulder*] Dear fool!

Count. I presume that the State could only go better, Sire, if we changed clothes. Though these steel corselets are rather heavy, they suit a king's body better than velvet.

King. Count, I came without attendants to your manor, to flee a mortal enemy who pursues your king determinedly, especially at court. We can fight and defeat him. Help me.

Count. You won't be deceived in your hope, Sire. Here's my arm and here's my sword. . . . We'll march towards him when you wish.

King. Not at all. We'll flee him.

Count. [*Making a movement.*] Who is he, then?

King. [*In the Count's ear.*] Boredom.

Count. [*Coldly.*] I thought, my lord—perhaps I was right—that your hurry to come could have been born of the desire to know if John VI had accepted the treaty which King Charles offered to him, which Charles of Savoisy took from Rennes to Brittany.

King. My poor ambassador, I admit it to my shame—I had, for my part, forgotten your departure by the time I learned of your return.

Count. But you come here, at least, for some important reason?

King. Of course.

Count. In that case, I suppose you have new interests that you
will entrust me with?

King. [*Mysteriously.*] Count, I come to hunt deer in your
forest — I have no more in mine.

Count. [*Half aloud.*] May my lord Saint Charles have pity on
us!

King. [*Crossly.*] I like people to speak up when they talk to me.
You said . . . ?

Count. That truly, sire, one could not lose a throne more gaily.
. . . But permit me at least, sire, to remind you . . .

Agnes. [*Appearing at the door.*] Are you coming, my lord?

King. [*Laughing.*] Agnes calls me, as you see.

Count. [*Begging.*] Just one moment!

King. The laws of hospitality decree that you should leave
your guest entirely free. . . . Goodnight.

Scene VII

Count. [*Alone.*] Yes, go sleep in your mistress' arms so that if
the cries of France in distress come during your nights to
make you start up from your sleep, a voice from hell
speaks to you even more loudly! Take up your chain,
woven with so much art that the slave himself does not
perceive it. Go — it would be rebellion if you were late.
Weak stag. . . . who could have been a lion.

[ANDREW *passes with some archers that he puts as sentinels in the courtyard.*]

Sleep, and I will myself watch over your sleep; because
our highest hope still lives in you alone. And God
wouldn't have put the kingdom in your hands if you
didn't suit his secret plans. Perhaps tomorrow, when I
will show the iron of this sword to your deceived soul as
a mirror, you will deny that the blade reflects the king,
recoiling in spite of yourself from the sudden image. The
torch isn't dead as long as a glimmer shines. My hand will
protect its wavering flame and I will keep away all winds
that could be fatal to it. And I will put the torch on the altar; one day, perhaps its pure brightness will shine! [*The
hour strikes. He listens.*] Midnight. Sleep peacefully, my
noble master. Our eyes will be open even if you sleep.
Keep watch, sentinels! [*A second sentinel can be heard, taking up the cry.*] Keep watch, sentinels!

[*The same cry is heard going off into the distance, until
it is too far away to be heard. The curtain falls.*]

ACT III

Scene I

[*It is day. The* Count *is standing guard at the king's door;* Andrew *at the other door. The sound of a horn can be heard as the curtain rises.*]

Count. Andrew, what's that noise?

Andrew. The horn.

Count. Who sounds?

Andrew. I can't see from here. It's outside.

Count. Then no one's at the drawbridge?

Andrew. Oh, yes, my lord; I put two men in the tower — Ah! it's friends of ours — They're opening. . . . I knew the guard was good. Ah! It's a squire who bears the arms of Narbonne. He's devilishly hot!

Count. Make a sign to them to bring him here at once.

Andrew. My lord, he's here. Come in, squire.

Squire. The count. . . .

Count. That's me.

Squire. [*Giving him a letter with the arms of Narbonne.*] Count, we need a prompt answer to the message. It's from my master.

Count. Alright. . . . You come back from the camp?

Squire. Yes, my lord.

Count. [*Reading.*] Narbonne does well?

Squire. Yes.

Count. When did you leave it?

Squire. Last night.

Count. By Saint Charles! That's quick walking. Your master speaks to me like a man who's hard-pressed. I can't rejoin him tomorrow, though.

Squire. He's waiting for the battle that the English offer. But he's considering. If he had help from your good lance and from all your archers he wouldn't hesitate any more.

Count. I have things that I absolutely must do during the next two days. Then I'll rejoin him. He must wait. That's possible — two days' wait can't be harmful, when he'll lose all with too much haste.

Squire. My lord, he told me to leave as soon as you gave me an answer.

Count. You'll have it in an hour at the latest. Go. Andrew, you stay. My friends, take care of this good squire. [*The squire leaves with the others.*] [*To Andrew.*] Andrew, today I have need of all your zeal.

Andrew. Give your orders

Count. You know the castle of Graville?

Andrew. Of course, my lord. It's near the city of Auxerre.

Count. Just so.

Andrew. When the Count—may God have mercy on his soul—was alive, by God, I made the same trip twenty times at your orders. That poor Count! He was killed in the defeat at Crévent. I brought the news. I seem to still hear his daughter say, with her sweet voice . . .

Count. Alright. Then you know Isabelle?

Andrew. Yes, my lord; and how beautiful she is!

Count. That's possible. I've never seen her. Well, Andrew, you will leave—and bring her this.

Andrew. This wedding ring!

Count. This wedding ring.

Andrew. But what shall I say to her?

Count. That you've come to get her in order to bring her to my home, that today I wait for her to come without delay. You understand me—today—because I'm leaving tomorrow evening.

Andrew. Alright.

Count. Respect her as your mistress, and call her "Countess" when you speak to her.

Andrew. I'll do as you say, my lord.

Count. Good.

Andrew. Do you have any other orders for me?

Count. No, nothing. Except to send the Saracen to me . . . [*Stopping.*] Listen! . . . I thought . . . it's nothing.

[*Looking at Berengaria's apartment on the side.*] Nothing but a sigh, no doubt . . . Go.

Andrew. The Saracen passed the night there; sleeping in his burnoose.[12]

Count. Let him come here.

Andrew. [*Calling him.*] Hey, you! What are you doing with your eyes fixed on the Countess' window, slave? Really!

Yacoub. [*On the threshold.*] Here I am, master.

Count. Come. Yesterday a sentence was passed against you — and you deserved it.

Yacoub. Yes, master.

Count. You were saved by a word from the King. Do you want to watch the door of your saviour for a moment this morning?

Yacoub. I really don't care where I stay, where I go, or where I'm coming from.

Count. So, Yacoub, you will stay here faithfully?

Yacoub. Yes, master.

Count. If the King suddenly appears, you'll withdraw to the other door.

Yacoub. Yes, master.

Count. I'll come back soon to relieve you. [*He leaves.*]

---

[12] The BURNOOSE is a kind of hooded cloak worn by the Arabs.

Yacoub. [*Alone, in thought.*] Why did she watch the whole
night long, like me, without closing her eyes an instant?
I thought that I alone watched over the stones. . . . I
saw her for an instant. . . . her tears flowed. . . . Her
tears! All my blood, Mohammed, for her sorrows! Life is
bad, then, to others, just as to me. Others suffer. . . .

Scene II

[YACOUB; BERENGARIA, *lifting the tapestry, and making sure that Yacoub is alone.*]

Beren. Yacoub!

Yacoub. [*Trembling and raising his head.*] Oh! How pale you are!

Beren. It's nothing. . . . I've been ill. . . .

Yacoub. You. . . . ill!

Beren. Why not? Each has his part of sorrow in this world.

Yacoub. You didn't sleep at all?

Beren. No. But I saw you standing like a shadow. I recognized
you though the night was dark. What were you doing?

Yacoub. The same thing I did last night. But you slept last
night and didn't see me. How many times, madam, like
a stag at bay who weeps and bells, haven't I passed long
nights at that same spot, with sobs and cries; following a
shadow passing on your stained glass windows; beating
my breast and saying: "Berengaria."

Beren. And why do you look for my shadow with your eyes,
in your tears and your forlornness? Why say my name?

Yacoub. Why does the sailor, on a cloudless night, fix his glance on a single star? Why does he say, between clenched teeth, a name he has already said a thousand times? It's because it's sweet to complain, even when it's hopeless. It's because he knows his arms can't stretch to the sky to reach it, but low as he is he can at least die with his eyes still fixed on that golden star.

Beren. Yes, Yacoub, I understand. Hidden from all eyes a flame exists in the depths of your soul. . . . During your first days, on the shores of the Nile, no doubt a voice promised eternal love to you. And you shut up the expression of that cherished voice and guarded it in your heart as in a sanctuary; and every night in the shadows it comes to talk to you quietly. And perhaps my voice, though foreign to it, resembles it.

Yacoub. That's it, Berengaria! [*Bitterly.*] You've guessed it.

Beren. But in your turn, you. . . . Yacoub, you must have promised her in return. . . .

Yacoub. I promised nothing. [*Staring at Berengaria.*] But I could promise what one asked for with her voice.

Beren. But one might ask too much, and then. . . .

Yacoub. Listen: If that voice bids me stay, or go; be sad or happy; strike or have mercy — whether her voice begs me or threatens me, all of its orders shall be performed just as well as just one was yesterday, when it said: "Live!"

Beren. And what would you demand in return for such submission?

Yacoub. How to "demand" from the one who holds you in their power? I would demand nothing. I would wait on my knees for her to say to me: "Good. Now, arise."

Beren. If, more justly, however, she left a gage of her faith in your hands, which she pledged in her turn . . .

Yacoub. To me? A gage of her faith, you said? Oh, you mock me, madam. Have pity on me!

Beren. [*Letting her glove fall.*] Pick up that glove for me.

[*While Yacoub bends, Berengaria lets the tapestry fall and closes her apartment door. At the same instant, the King and Agnes appear in the door on the other side.*]

Yacoub. [*Rising.*] Here it is. . . . [*Looking and searching for Berengaria in vain.*] Heaven and earth! She's disappeared. Just now she was. . . . Berengaria! Berengaria! This glove left between my hands. . . . [*He kisses it in a transport. He sees the King and Agnes.*] She feared they saw her, that's all. . . . I'm a madman.

Scene III

[Yacoub; King; Agnes]

King. Agnes, what are you looking at from the window, and what makes you smile?

Agnes. Oh! My lord! Master! Look with me for a moment at the sun in the sky—so brilliant that it makes you lower your eyes. Well, it was veiled by a cloud when it rose. You could barely discern its passage there. All the earth was sad and cold; it seemed that the world barely woke today, that everything was suffering; faded; soulless; waiting for a ray of its flame in order to live—That's how all is reborn or all dies without it. Well, my sweet lord, today when I saw it victorious over cloud and shadow I thought that, if your morning has been dark, as it was, a day must come also when the radiant brightness of your forehead will cause eyes to be lowered. Because he was already ravished from the earth—[*Shows Yacoub.*]—but you appeared, and returned him to life.

King. Ah! yes. . . . I recognize the condemned slave.

Agnes. Let's speak to him. Do you wish it?

King. [*Gesturing to Yacoub.*] In what place were you born?

Yacoub. Far from here.

King. But what do they call your country?

Yacoub. The desert.

Agnes. The desert?

King. Yes. That's in Syria. Alain Chartier[13] often spoke to me of a country far away, in the East, where holy King Louis[14] went to wage war. Slave, you remember a king who conquered you—a pious and good king—

Yacoub. My ancestor told my father that one day a nazarite[15] chief disembarked at the port of Abu Mandour, leading

---

[13] ALAIN CHARTIER (1385-1433) was a poet and writer who served as secretary to both Charles VI and Charles VII. His most famous poem was "La Belle Dame sans mercy" (1424). He also wrote the "Quadrilogue invectif" (1422), an appeal, in prose, for unity among the French.

[14] HOLY KING LOUIS is Saint Louis, or Louis IX. He set sail for Tunis in 1270, on the Eighth Crusade, but died of the plague at Carthage along with many of his troops. He was canonized a few years after his death.

[15] NAZARITE is an Arab term meaning "Christian." Some disrespect is implied.

galleys with sails more numerous than the stars are in the sky at night. They said they wanted to conquer the tomb of Jesus, whom they call the son of God, in the Holy Land. But Allah alone is great! At the voice of the Prophet the desert called the tempest to its aid. The *simoun* hurled itself upon them like a lion and wrapped them in its fiery wings. It was done. The immense and insurmountable desert covered their bones with its winding sheet of sand. The Nazarite chief perished there without renown; and the echo from Tunis did not tell me his name.

King. Well, Agnes; there's what they call glory. See what an impression it made on his memory! Perhaps, as my ancestor did, I also could have gone to search for a winding sheet in the desert and brought, following me, like a hecatomb, thirty thousand soldiers to die on my grave. And they would have said, here, that that was great and beautiful! But you see, I'd rather lie down in the tomb near the evening of a lovely day, my eyes fixed on my star, have for my winding sheet the cloth that veils you and find some friend who would sorrowfully write on my headstone, "Here lies Charles, loved by Agnes."

Agnes. My lord!

King. [*To Yacoub.*] Leave us.

[*Yacoub retires.*]

Isn't it true that life, which comes to us so slowly and is taken from us so quickly—this smile of God's, this heavenly favor—belongs to happiness, Agnes, and wasn't made in order to throw its days like smoke to that wind of pride that they call fame? Besides, Agnes, what do they call happiness down here? Could it be, by chance, the chimerical honor of waking up as a child on the steps of a throne; of tiring one's forehead with the weight of a crown; of seeing courtiers eager to do Our will; of never speaking without saying, "I wish it!" No, isn't it true, Agnes, that happiness is the joy of your sweet looks drowning me a thousand times a day; it's my tired forehead bending under yours; it's your lowered breath mingling itself with mine — it's this warm shudder gliding into my very heart; it's the sound of your voice saying "I love you."

Agnes. As long as you love me you'll think so. . . . My sweet lord.

King. I'm the one who's at your mercy. Why can't I bury my days with you in deep peace in some corner of the world? For sometimes I can hardly get my wits together and I feel my reason become confused. . . . I think of my father only with trembling![16] What do they want of me, with their battle cries? Why not leave my sword in my sheath? I already had enough of blood at Montereau![17]

Agnes. My lord, rest your head on my breast.

King. Do you think a tempest is gathering in the sky? The horizon is darkening.

Agnes. No.

King. The air seems heavy to me. Don't you hear a muffled roaring in the distance? Listen! [*One hears the sound of cannon.*]

---

[16] " . . . my father . . . " Charles VII's father, Charles VI, went mad in 1392. Lack of a strong government in France after this time was a factor in the ensuing civil war and invasion.

[17] MONTEREAU. John the Fearless, Duke of Burgundy, was assassinated on the bridge at Montereau in 1419 by the Dauphin's advisers.

Agnes. My lord, let the storm scold. When I hold you like this—Oh! my courage is great—because lightening can't strike one of us without killing the other also.

Scene IV

[*The preceding. The* COUNT *brusquely opens the door to the rear.*]

Count. Wake up, sire!

Agnes. Ah!

King. Who comes here without my orders? Is it you, my host? The servants in this castle fail in their duties, when one can come into the presence of the king without being announced.

[*The sound of cannon.*]

Count. Sire, listen to that noise. It comes, like me, without fear of your power, to say to you as I do: "Sire, awake!"

King. Isn't it the sound of thunder?

Count. No.

King. No?

Count. Listen again.

King. Ah! . . . .

Count. It's the voice of the cannon!

King. Well?

Count. Well! I say that that voice which speaks ought to find an echo in King Charles' heart; that he has been sleeping a deep sleep for a long time and if he wants to finally wake up, the time's come!

King. Count!

Count. I also say that every man who falls says, throwing a last look around him before being laid bloody in the tomb: "At this moment I die for him—where's the king?" Your ancestors got us into the habit of seeing their helmets shine wherever things were most difficult, and few blows with sword or with dagger fell, in which their royal shields had no part. Sire, it's agony for a people to think, while dying, that their king has disowned them, because they may, thinking themselves released from their oath, be seized with the desire also to disown their king. In these times of agony, who can bind so many powerful and jealous lords together, as if in a sheaf, rallying around our monarchy, if not the king, first lord of all? Can't each think that God will pardon him for abandoning the king, when the king abandons himself?

King. Count you forget

Count. And sire, I also say that it's not wise to waste your treasure in bells for your falcons and jewels for your mistresses, when it's drenched with the sweat of your people—each piece. Those are vain luxuries that it would be better to suppress while there's no gold to buy iron! If I remember well, the ancient French state grew in territory under each of its kings. The kings added more to the ancient patrimony than they were bequeathed. Philip of Valois conquered Champagne after the Dauphinée.[18]

---

[18] PHILIP OF VALOIS (Philip VI, 1293–1350) is actually the king who lost the battle of Crecy to the English at the beginning of the Hundred Years' War and had to cede Calais to them. However, he did buy the province of Dauphinée, incorporating it into France.

Philip Augustus, rejecting Brittany from afar, took Normandy, Maine and Anjou.[19] He opened Poitou with the key of Tours. Louis IX[20] added Languedoc to France by a treaty. As son–in–law of Louis of Anjou,[21] you yourself had the rights to Provence. . . .

King. By God! And if I, in my turn, remember well, I hold this state of France, my lord Count, from God. And I don't have to account for it, therefore, except to God. If it pleases me to abandon it entirely, none will judge me but God.

Count. I say that, of France as her princes made her, only three provinces yet remain to you, Sire. The victorious English are invading with large steps, and John VI, their ally, traps and deceives you. With big gulps Philip of Burgundy devours your counties of Argmagnac, Foix and Bigorre. Don't you see them, sire, surrounding you, coming step by step to swallow you up? Your troops, closed in by a living mesh, can't sustain the shock of three armies. Poton, Xaintraille, Narbonne and Dunois[22] strike in vain, without letting themselves tire, as in a tourney, attacking without plans, retreating, but not in unison—a day disperses those who are hardly reassembled in a month. They have arms to strike and resolute hearts, but they lack a chief; soul and center of all. Sire, it would be a disgrace to your name to wait any longer to join them.

---

[19] PHILIP AUGUSTUS (1165–1223) took Normandy from King John of England in 1202–4, and acquired the provinces of Auvergne (1201) and Champagne (1213). A contemporary of Richard the Lion-Hearted, he is considered one of the great French kings.

[20] LOUIS IX (see above). By the treaty of Paris in 1259, he acquired Normany, Maine, Anjou, and Poitou from the English.

[21] LOUIS OF ANJOU. Charles VII would have had the rights to any lands his wife inherited from her father.

[22] These are the names of generals fighting on Charles VII's side.

King. Count—has Our forest of Auxerre been seized?

Count. No.

King. We're going to hunt there. Prepare your falcon. Agnes, come.

Scene V

[COUNT, AGNES]

Count. [*Stopping Agnes*] No. No, Madam—you stay, because it's your turn to hear me. Oh, woman! You're beautiful. Oh, yes—beautiful, and I understand the power your black eyes have over your weak lover. You have the voice of an angel, or an enchantress, and I even understand how you can give orders, as mistress—But on my honor, it would be better for you if a red-hot iron put out that voice and those eyes—

Agnes. Oh! What are you saying to me?

Count. —because Frenchmen owe the misery of France to their power. And Charles—that madman—submits himself to their law as if to God. A king's mistress can become the demon of a people, or their angel, from the elevated sphere where her power places her. You could have been the angel of France. But you preferred to be her demon! Yes, the west has its Sardanapalus[23] now thanks to your adulterous and fatal love. The feeble monarchy struggles strangling in your embraces, in its last moments. Well— when it falls under the blows your hand is giving to it and is believed to be dead, and the English come to divide its

---

[23] SARDANAPALUS was an Assyrian king, famous for his debauchery. He, his concubines, and his treasure were all destroyed in a pyre.

remains—that's when cries will pursue you everywhere. You'll flee—but a kingdom struggles in agony much longer than a man does. Our cities all on fire will be your torches, and your feet will hit a tomb at every step—You'll flee—you'll flee without anything stopping you, because you won't know where to lay your head anymore.

Agnes. Mercy! Mercy!

Count. Those of our sons who remain will follow you with cries when they see you pass. The dying will open their eyes again, and raise themselves up in their beds in order to curse you in their last hour. The voice of your heart will join itself to their voices and all will cry out to you— "Curses be on you! Curses!"

Agnes. [*on her knees*] My lord, there's nothing that repentance can't erase. All this won't happen, my lord. Mercy! Mercy! Oh! Things aren't yet as bad as you believe—and the hand that made the wound can cure it.

Count. Try!

ACT IV

[*All the gear for a hunt. Pages at the door, holding dogs on leashes.*]

Scene I

[BALTHAZAR; GODFREY, *with a falcon on his wrist; peasants in the background; then,* YACOUB.]

Balthazar. [*At the door.*] Ho, there! Squires, bring out the gear. You pages, stop tormenting the hounds like that. . .They will have enough to do today, and if they're already three-quarters tired out before they leave they'll give up the track as soon as they dart forth . . . Bring the falcons and put hoods on all of them, so that none of them can see. . . . [*To Godfrey, taking away the falcon, which he's teasing.*] Here, Godfrey – go away! No matter what their lineage, if we leave these noble animals in the hands of these sons of Belial, the hounds won't follow the scent for forty paces, and the falcons, bewildered by them, will flee like goshawks before a cormorant. [*to someone else*] Do you think that we have enough lures for the day? Go get more. John, we'll leave in an hour. [*Speaking to his falcon.*] Haw! Haw! Come kiss me, Coquette. Oh, don't you want to – you king's favorite? We'll see if you're as proud this evening when we take you to dine.

Peasant. Master Pierre. . . .

Balthazar. Well?

Peasant. When I crossed the thicket this morning, I saw a boar pass on the road.

Balthazar. What size?

Peasant. Short and thickset. He had defenses that could unstitch ten hounds.

Balthazar. Saint Hubert!²⁴ And you think we could still find him now?

Peasant. Certainly. I would guarantee it.

Balthazar. That's good. Thanks, churl. Oh, why don't I have my good English bloodhound, to divert it! [*To Yacoub, who comes in and takes his accustomed place on his tiger–skin.*] Is that you, snowball? Will you follow us?

Yacoub. No.

Balthazar. The coward would rather lie down. [*He turns and sees a child touching a bow.*] You monkey bastard, are you tired of touching that bow! Stop it! Or I'll caress your back with this rope, without mercy.

Scene II

[*The preceding; the* KING.]

King. Shall we have a good hunt today, Balthazar?

Balthazar. Dam! I really don't know, sire. It's all up to chance. I remember one day. . . .

King. [*Ruffling the falcon.*] Ah! Are you there, Coquette?

---

²⁴ SAINT HUBERT is the patron saint of hunters.

Balthazar. [*Continuing.*]. . . . when we were on the trail in the late morning. . . .

King. [*Without listening to him.*] We're late.

Balthazar. [*Continuing.*] It was in the forest of Verneuil. We left. . . .

King. Is the Count ready?

Balthazar. We haven't seen him.

King. But where's our host?

Balthazar. [*Continuing.*] I let my falcon go. . . .

King. Has Agnes also neglected to come?

Balthazar. . . . at a plover . . .

King. Balthazar, take your horn and sound the departure. [*Balthazar sounds.*] Good.

Balthazar. [*Lively.*] I see it still. I don't think it had flapped its wings thirty times . . .

King. Here—hold Coquette.

Balthazar. Ah! come, girl.

King. [*Going to the door.*] You caused a miracle with your horn. Here's the count coming in at last. [*Looking, and trying to distinguish who's with him.*] With . . .

Scene III

[*The preceding; the* COUNT; JOHN, BASTARD OF ORLEANS[25]]

John. [*Entering.*] John of Orleans!

King. Dunois!. . . . my dear Dunois! By God, when I wish for something, the very thing arrives! [*He strikes him on the shoulder.*]

John. Sire—I'm grateful for your warm welcome, but if you would strike more lightly, please . . . [*He takes off his helmet. It can be seen that he has received a head wound which is still bleeding.*]

King. [*Recoiling.*] Blood! Oh, brave Dunois!

John. It's a scratch. But, by St. John! It's a good thing that I have a hard head. A serf would have had his forehead split open.

King. Indeed! You come from fighting, then?

John. Yes, my lord. Violently.

King. Well, before the battle, you should have brought Xaintraille here to hunt with us.

John. Xaintraille's been captured.

---

[25] The historical JOHN, BASTARD OF ORLEANS, COUNT OF DUNOIS (1403–68) was the illegitimate son of Louis I, Duke of Orleans. He fought at the side of Joan of Arc when Joan convinced Charles VII to put her at the head of an army in 1429, and was instrumental in many of her victories over the English. The historical Charles, contrary to the impression given in this play, did nothing to regain his own throne until aided by this great woman general—and did not attempt to save her when she was captured, tried, and executed by the English.

King. Xaintraille—a captive!

John. They've set his ransom.

King. Ho, there! Treasurer! What still remains in your poor purse?

Treasurer. Eleven hundred golden pieces.

King. [*To John.*] Hold out your helmet, if that's the sum he needs.

John. He needs even more. His ransom is two thousand gold pieces. [*The king turns to his treasurer.*]

Treasurer. Sire, if I have even one more, may heaven abandon me!

King. [*Taking off his hat, on which is a crown.*] See which is the most beautiful of the diamonds set in my crown.

Treasurer. This one shines most.

King. [*Breaking the setting and throwing the diamond in Dunois' helmet.*] My most beautiful diamond for my best soldier.

Count. Oh! I knew his heart was good!

King. Ask Narbonne to arrange the ransom. Later he'll give me an account of the time and place.

John. Sire, he's arranging his own accounts, at this moment—with God.

King. Dead!

John. Dead. Narbonne attacked this morning against the advice of Douglas and Xaintraille. He didn't survive his mistake.

King. God have mercy. I hope Douglas is safe and sound?

John. He's dead, too.

King. Oh, my poor Douglas! My faithful ally—you who came from Scotland[26] to embrace my quarrel—to see you die for me! I'm an unhappy man! D'Aumale, Rambouillet, Vantadour?

John. Dead, like them.

King. Lafayette and Gaucourt?

John. Captive.

King. And the army?

John. Ask for smoke from an extinguished fire!

King. Destroyed!

John. Dispersed; and on each side, each surviving captain retreats in haste from Bedford the conqueror, as best he can. Only the king could rally them.

Agnes. [*Coming near the king.*] Farewell, sire.

King. Where are you going, Agnes?

Agnes. I'm leaving.

King. You!. . . .

Agnes. My lord, a gypsy once foretold that I should have this honor—and I've kept the hope of it for some time—he said

---

[26] Scotland was not part of the United Kingdom at this time but a separate nation, often at war with England, and glad to help her enemies.

I'd have the love of the King of France. My forewarned heart, believing in the law alone, thought until now that you were king. But Bedford takes the title and the rank from you, and since Your Highness cedes them without combat, Bedford is the only king of France. And here I am—ready to join Bedford.

King. Oh. It's like that. Come here, Count. Do you have a war-horse fit for a king to ride?

Count. I have my father's.

King. Let it be brought here to me this instant.

Count. [*To his squire.*] Obey the king, sir squire.

King. Thank you. Do you have armor in this castle that would fit me, worthy of a king on a day of battle?

Count. [*Showing him the suits of armor.*] You see, sire.

King. Good. The strongest is for me.

Count. Take down this armor and arm the king.

[*From this line until the words, "Dunois, my spurs," the Count's servants put armor on the King.*]

King. I wish to know the results of your mission now. Tell me.

Count. Sire, I saw John VI.

King. Well? I'm listening.

Count. He promised me he'd break a treaty made with your enemies, and sign an act of alliance with you, for peace or war, and that he'd send his brother to the French camp with a thousand men. That's his offer.

King. That's good. What does he want in return?

Count. He asks the constable's sword for his brother, Rich-mond, taken from Boukent who escaped at Crévent.

King. Is that all?

Count. Yes, sire.

King. He'll receive it from your hand, Count. You'll go tomor-row and you'll bring him my royal word that, on my part at least, the alliance is loyal. Let him go to Poitiers. We'll join him there.

Count. Sire, I'll go.

King. Dunois, my spurs. [*Dunois puts on the king's spurs.*] A sword now. [*The Count gives him one. The king looks at it.*] Count, a sword for the hand of a king must be tempered more strongly than this one is. This one would break — See — [*He breaks it.*] — at the first blows my arm struck. [*The Count gives him another.*] This one is good. [*To a squire who carries a lance.*] The Saracen shall be my lance-bearer. Give this to him. . . . My helmet. . . . [*They give it to him. He puts it on the table.*] And now, silence! Until now I thought to obtain an honorable peace from Bedford by se-cret treaties. This means seems too slow and vulgar to all of you. You ask for war. . . .

All. [*Throwing themselves on the armor.*] Yes! War! War!

King. Well! Support me in a last effort — then you will have it, children — war to the death! I pulled out my sword after all France did — my sword will be the last to be resheathed. You wish me for chief? Well — here are my commands. Philip Augustus' France — the France of the Valois — that's not mine. I need the France whose limits Charlemagne traced in the heart of Germany, when the giant touched, as sovereign master, the Rhine with one hand and the ocean with the other. Let my will, my lords, be yours— because that's my France—mine. I don't know of any other.

John. Sire, we listen to your orders on our knees.

· *King.* Henceforth let us all utter one cry! We'll see who in the combat urges loudest—"Mountjoy and St. Dennis! Charles to the rescue!"

All. Mountjoy and St. Dennis! Charles to the rescue!

King. And now, Agnes, say who is king. Come falconers, to the hunt! Follow me.

[*He leaves. All follow.*]

Count. [*To Dunois.*] Don't abandon him—and moderate the flame of this first transport. [*To Agnes.*] Honor to you, madam!

Agnes. Honor to God alone, Count, who opened this path for me. To God, who holds the hearts of princes in his hand! [*They leave together.*]

Balthazar. [*Alone for a moment.*] Well, our hunt will vary today. The Englishman is game of high venery, but since some blow might fall on his hunters, Coquette, we're going to return you to your perch.

[*He starts to leave.*]

Scene IV

[BALTHAZAR; BERENGARIA, *raising the door-curtain.*]

Beren. Falconer. . . .

Balthazar. Noble lady. . . .

Beren. Is the Count leaving with the King to go to the army? I couldn't hear clearly, shut up in that apartment. I must know immediately if he's leaving.

Balthazar. Yet they spoke loudly.

Beren. But is he leaving? Is he leaving? Oh! on your soul! Answer me—is he leaving right now?

Balthazar. No, madam. He stays tonight; he won't leave until tomorrow.

Beren. [*Giving him a purse.*] There—for you.

Balthazar. God bless your hand!

Beren. [*Alone.*] Oh! I feel the blood rushing back to my heart. . . . I'm strangling between these walls, as if in a tomb. . . . [*falling into an armchair*] I had thought he was leaving—Oh, how I suffer! It's as if someone squeezed me in two iron hands. . . . [*Standing up suddenly.*] My God! Come to my aid! Here he is!

Scene V

[BERENGARIA; *the* COUNT.]

Count. [*Astonished.*] Berengaria!

Beren. I've already become such a stranger to you today that
you're surprised to see me? In that case, forgive me, my
lord, but I had thought . . . perhaps I was wrong . . .
[*The Count makes a movement of impatience.*] If it pleases you
to tell me whether I should speak or keep silent . . .

Count. Speak.

Beren. I had thought, then, I say, that before burying my days
in a living tomb, and permitting that the bond between us
blessed by God, and consecrated by the Church be broken forever, I could have come before you, when this dis-
honor burst forth on me, and said: "My lord, what I have
done that, using all your strength in this way, you want
to shrivel me with this shameful divorce?" The judge at
least tells the accused what heinous crime he has committed. . . . Before punishing me tell me, my judge, what
have I done?

Count. Berengaria; the person whose forsworn mouth insulted you with a single suspicion would see my glove,
with a denial, fall at his feet immediately, telling him of
his mistake. No—the most pure and faithful woman could
still take you for a model—I know it. There's no duty im-
posed on your sex that it doesn't seem easy for you to ac-
complish, and the Lord in heaven guards a place for you
among his angels, to sing his praises at their side. But a
man who's chained by the rank I hold accepts duties
greater than yours; and although these duties often are a
torment, when the time comes he must fulfill them. He
struggles a long time to keep his happiness, but everything comes to shatter itself against the word "honor."
Now the honor of France and the honor of my lineage
both demand that a child replace me one day so that, sus-
taining the renown of both, he should fight for her, and
transmit my name. Berengaria; that is all.

Beren. Yes, I know it. But Charles—do you believe that pride alone speaks to me in my heart? Ah, no. No. Love speaks to me more than that. Just as strongly today as it did on the first day when I answered "Yes," when your beloved voice said to me, "Do you take me for your husband, Berengaria?" Oh, you said it, that's the truth. Man, tormented by a thousand petty cares, keeps little place for love in his heart, and that's accepted, but woman! Woman, who has no happiness to hope for in this world but that which comes from her lord and master whom she formerly made an oath to love forever, at his prayer. She keeps this oath and loves him. When he comes suddenly one day to order her to extinguish her love, because he doesn't love her anymore, the poor woman should be forgiven, alas! for not being able to blow out the flame in her heart after having guarded it ten years like a treasure. Charles, forgive me for still loving you!

Count. Oh—even if his life were a crime, I would wish to have a child, whoever he was, to inherit my name, even if he had to bear the bar of illegitimacy[27] on his shield, so that my name wouldn't die entirely with me. Even if, to expiate his fatal birth, I had to bury the rest of my days in a cloister!

Beren. Listen. Sometimes God wants to test our hearts. And when they come victorious out of the test, his anger gives place to his mercy and he gives us that which he long refused. Wait a while before sending me away from you. Wait—and God will have pity on me.

---

[27] BAR OF ILLEGITIMACY (or bar sinister). An illegitimate son of a noble house acknowledged by the family would have the family arms on his shield marked with a black bar.

Count. Wait — in the midst of the hazards of a deadly war! And will death wait to strike?

Beren. Death! Oh, my lord, I will pray so much for you that the angel of battle will ward off the blows. Isn't there somewhere that I can go on a holy pilgrimage? Whatever the journey, I will make it — even in unknown places, at the other end of the world!

Count. Child!

Beren. I will go barefoot! Where the sun burns or the tempest growls I'll go without asking for shelter for my head; I'll go crying, praying, a rosary in my hand; and I won't sleep until the journey's end!

Count. In heaven's name call back your reason which is leaving you!

Beren. Tell me, my lord, do you wish me to go?

Count. It's impossible.

Beren. And why?

Count. I've spoken.

Beren. You won't consider this action then? It's my damnation! You're sending me away in order to take another wife — Isn't it so? Isn't it so? Well, I'm jealous. Oh! What will it be then when even to the altar when I wish to pray, the fatal word comes that another is your wife! Oh, my lord, I fear that I will mix prayers and blasphemy together and, in my despair, call the anger of God on me, on her — and perhaps on you!

Count. God gives strength to those he afflicts.

Beren. Even the power of God, when He does miracles, can
be exercised on the future alone. The future is His, but not
the past. Whatever His supreme power is, can He cause
it to be that your voice hasn't said to me, "I love you!" and
that the still victorious accent of that voice isn't living at
this moment in my heart? I know well that He can, if He
wishes, make me mad, to cause me to forget that sound,
that word—and take the memory away from me. But I
don't believe that He can prevent that those words were
said to me a hundred times! Remember those words,
Charles, I beg you. Look—I'm crying and humbling myself at your feet. . . . Oh, don't look away from me! Oh,
have mercy, my lord!. . . .

Count. [*Taking her by the arm.*] Get up. It's too late.

Beren. I called prayer to my aid first, looking for pity from your
stony heart. Soon you saw the excess of my sorrow burst
out in sobs and pour itself out in tears. Finally, with my
head dishevelled I threw myself at your feet and rolled
about. What more do you want? Is there something I can
do? Speak! Speak, if you're a Christian! Answer this poor
woman! Don't leave her with death in her soul. Console
her, weep with her, give her a word of love . . . just
one . . . Oh, be accursed!

[*The Count rings. A servant appears.*]

Count. The chaplain.

Beren. [*Going into her room.*] Farewell. Your hands dig my
tomb. My lord, pray to God that I'm the only one who
falls into it.

Scene VI

[*The* COUNT, *alone; then* YACOUB *and the* CHAPLAIN.]

Count. Alright. Be ready to leave in a moment when the Chaplain comes to give you word. I can brave your hate better than your love . . . Is that you, Chaplain?

[*He turns, and sees Yacoub.*]

Yacoub, who brings you back?

Yacoub. Because I was given as one gives a dog, I broke my leash like a dog and I've returned. But today the dog can serve as a model for the master—because the master is ungrateful and the dog is faithful.

[*He takes his accustomed place.*]

Count. Stay here, since you like it better. [*To the Chaplain, who enters.*] You're here, Sir Chaplain, thank God! Berengaria is preparing to leave this castle.

[*Yacoub listens with attention.*]

You'll accompany her to whatever convent she has chosen for her retreat, sir. You'll make a pledge to the abbess, in my name, to pay a dowry more rich[28] and more sure than a queen would pay upon entering . . . And then you'll return, since I'm waiting for Isabelle this evening, and leaving tomorrow. Time is measured out for me with a stingy hand, now—Therefore, make haste, father. [*To a servant.*] Prepare a gentle palfrey. Wait here, sir . . . I'll leave so that she can pass.

---

[28] One paid a DOWRY upon entering a convent, just as one did at marriage. A nun, of course, was supposed to be married to Christ.

Yacoub. Allah! [*He rises and goes to the Count.*] Master?

Count. What now?

Yacoub. Yesterday you offered to return a benefit to me that God alone has the right to take from us—Freedom. Do you still wish to give it to me? I hadn't properly added up the price of this treasure when I refused it.

Count. Since I offered it to you, let it be restored to you. [*He takes a parchment from the table, applies his seal to it, then gives it to Yacoub.*] The thing I offered is granted. Farewell.

Yacoub. Thank you.

[*The Count leaves. The Chaplain goes to knock on Berengaria's door. She opens it, a veiled woman goes out of it, wearing a costume exactly like Berengaria's.*]

Chaplin. Daughter, put your tears at God's feet. Only God can console you. [*He withdraws with her.*]

Yacoub. [*Following this woman with his eyes.*] Farewell—you angel who came down from the eternal vault to touch my forehead with your wing and refresh it. You are certainly going to the abode of the happy ones. Mohammed calls you back to him.

Beren. [*From the threshold of her apartment.*] Yacoub!

Yacoub. [*Taking turns looking at the departing woman, and Berengaria calling him.*] There are two of them!

Beren. Yacoub . . . Well—is my voice strange to you?

Yacoub. Berengaria—is it you?

Beren. Myself.

Yacoub. Berengaria—you're staying here?

Beren. I'm staying here.

Yacoub. And who's leaving with the Chaplain then?

Beren. My servant.

Yacoub. Pardon . . . but you don't know . . .

Beren. I know everything.

Yacoub. That the Count . . .

Beren. Slave, I tell you that I know my shame.

Yacoub. What! You know that in a moment, another is going to come here?

Beren. What are you saying?

Yacoub. That the Count is waiting for her . . .

Beren. You're lying!

Yacoub. . . . that they're decorating the chapel for this evening . . .

Beren. You're lying!

Yacoub. . . . that Andrew is bringing her; calling her "Countess" in advance?

Beren. I tell you that you lie!

[*At this moment Isabelle arrives on horseback, led by Andrew to the door at the back of the courtyard. The Count goes to her and offers her a hand to help her down.*]

Yacoub. Well. So be it. [*Showing Isabelle and the Count to her.*] Look—what do you say to me now?

Beren. [*Overwhelmed.*] Nothing.

Yacoub. Nothing! Look again. He's kissing her.

Beren. Accursed!

Yacoub. And you say nothing.

Beren. [*With fury.*] I say that I'm in love with you! [*She tries to go back inside.*]

Yacoub. [*Restraining her.*] Stay. Stay. Stay.

Beren. The Count might see me.

Yacoub. When will I meet you again?

Beren. Here. This evening.

   [*She goes in.*]

Yacoub. This evening!

ACT V

Scene I

[*The archers, eating;* YACOUB, *standing near Berengaria's door.*]

An Archer: By God, the venison is good.

Andrew. It's perfect. I didn't suspect when I brought this buck back to the castle yesterday morning, that for such a celebration. . . . Have a bit, Yacoub; let bygones be bygones.

Yacoub. I'm not hungry.

An Archer: [*To Andrew.*] Well! You're in the master's favor now. You'll look after us.

Andrew. You're making fun of me. But perhaps it is something, though, sirs, to have been chosen by my lord Charles of Savoisy to bring his wife back to this castle. I hope that a new marriage will make him a father at last—and that I will not go on such an errand a second time. On that note, I drink to the young Countess!

All. We do, too! We do, too!

Yacoub. Despicable wretches!

Andrew. Humph! What did you say?

Yacoub. I said that the men who are here now made a toast yesterday, encouraged by you yourself—only it was to another's health.

Andrew. Make your own toast, and we'll make ours.

Yacoub. I don't drink.

Andrew. Well, let us drink, then; and if we're disturbing you go take a turn outside.

Yacoub. It pleases me to stay.

Andrew. Stay, but by St. Charles! be quiet.

Yacoub. I still have something else to say.

Andrew. Speak.

Yacoub. Let a single one of you agree with this cursed toast and I'll break my glass between his teeth. I've spoken.

[*Andrew stands up to threaten Yacoub.*]

An Archer: [*To Andrew, in a low voice.*] Remember Raymond! [*The chimes are heard.*] We have to go to the chapel, Andrew; that sound is calling us. [*They go out.*]

Scene II

[Yacoub; *then* Berengaria.]

Yacoub. How slow you were to leave, you Giaours[29]. May Allah take as many days from your lives as you have taken

---

[29] GIAOURS. Arab word roughly equivalent to "devil." Dumas (and his readers) were probably familiar with it because of Byron's immensely popular poem, of that name, published in 1813.

moments of joy away from me by staying in this place, from which that sound sends you away. [*Raising the tapestry.*] Come, they aren't here anymore. Berengaria, come—Don't you hear me? [*Turning around.*] Damned Nazarites! Berengaria! Oh, my heart, swelling and bounding, is about to burst my breast!

Beren. [*Appearing.*] Silence!

Yacoub. It's you.

Beren. Are we alone?

Yacoub. Yes; alone.

Beren. Listen carefully. Put out the torches first.

Yacoub. They hear nothing. They're at the chapel, where the priest is uniting. . . .

Beren. Enough! Enough! Let's talk of something else. Perhaps, when you've wandered around this castle in the evenings, when you have long turned your eyes and thoughts towards the East in your despair, you've sat, and with a lowered head, your gaze obscured by a half sleep, at times you've dreamt something like this: You were in the desert, seated under your tent. You looked at the dazzling clouds in the distance, where the swollen sun swayed and fell asleep, in an ocean of gold, near the day's end . . . You heard the bells on the she-camels, always obedient to your voice, tinkle while they were milked; your faithful horses hastened—neighing. And seated near you, a foreign woman—the one called Berengaria in the West—twined amorous arms around your neck and asked, "Yacoub, are you happy?"

Yacoub. Do you think I can control myself when I hear this?

Beren. Perhaps you've dreamt like this? Tell me.

Yacoub. A thousand times! A thousand times!

Beren. And when some idiot passed by you with a sudden noise, breaking the charm, and when everything around you showed the lie of your dream—when you found yourself a slave again, naked and poor; if suddenly someone had unexpectedly appeared and made your strange dream, by the power of a demon or an angel, into a reality; and only asked for your obedience in return for one moment, one day—an obedience, though, which nothing could blunt, like that of iron in the hand which thrusts it—would you have hesitated to buy eternal happiness, at the price of that one moment?

Yacoub. One person only would have had the power to make my heart submit and obey. She that I see in that sweet dream—I have no need to say that it's you.

Beren. Well, listen then! Do you wish that dream to become real, some morning? Do you wish to find again your native desert; the caravan seated in the shade of the nopal; your light horses, changeable in running; your hundred camels sleeping around your tent; the Northern woman whose loving arms. . . .

Yacoub. You're going to ask for something dreadful, aren't you. It doesn't matter.

Beren. Yacoub, if your words aren't just frivolous sounds which escape you, you said these words to me: "If by chance there were some man whom it hurt you to look at—if his days had this influence on your days and if only his death could end your suffering—even if he had received the right to hurt you from Mohammed, it would only be necessary to point him out to me when he passed." You said that.

Yacoub. I said it. I tremble . . . But I made an exception of one man.

Beren. Of no one!

Yacoub. One man has the right to escape my vengeance.

Beren. If it was that man whom you had to strike? If vengeance on him had to be swift?

Yacoub. His name?

Beren. The Count!

Yacoub. By hell! I suspected it.

Beren. The Count, do you understand, the Count! Well . . .?

Yacoub. I can't.

Beren. Then farewell forever! . . .

Yacoub. Stay . . . or I'll follow you.

Beren. Until now I thought—what a foolish belief!—that only Christians broke their word. I was mistaken. That's all.

Yacoub. Madam!

Beren. Leave me. [*Turning.*] But you lied to me, then?

Yacoub. You well know why. My vengeance can't unite with yours. He saved my life. Oh! Name me any other . . .

Beren. And what other can I name, Yacoub, whose fatal power

has done you more harm for ten years now? Oh—do you
remember, do you remember . . .

Yacoub. Madam, I remember everything.

Beren. He caused you to lose your soul. You said it yourself.
He stole your country, parents, freedom, joy and love
from you forever. Every time he touches you he takes
away some happiness from you.

Yacoub. And that drop of water that he poured in my mouth?

Beren. If he saved your life, wasn't it in order to make you submit to a thousand deaths later? Slavery has restored the
balance between you. He has finally made you a slave!

Yacoub. [*Showing the Count's signature.*] He gives me freedom!

Beren. That's fine! And with freedom does he give back to you
my love, which he deprived you of for ten years?

Yacoub. Berengaria, listen to me for a moment . . .

Beren. I'm listening. Speak quickly!

Yacoub. I thought . . . no doubt I was mistaken . . . that
here you said . . . right here . . . forgive me . . .

Beren. What?

Yacoub. That you were in love with me.

Beren. Yes, I said it.

Yacoub. Well, then, since the same fate and same love bring
us together, Berengaria, this evening . . .

Beren. Well?

Yacoub. Let's flee together.

Beren. Without striking?

Yacoub. Won't his remorse avenge you?

Beren. You slave! Do you think my heart is set so low that in this world I can endure to have been the lover of two men, one right after the other, and that the first of them should insult me and both of them continue to live without the second avenging me on him? Can one love enter without destroying the other? If you hoped for that, the hope is insulting!

Yacoub. Berengaria!

Beren. All is finished between us. Get out!

Yacoub. Please . . .

Beren. I will know how to find some hand less timid and some soul less cowardly for this task, who will do for money what you have not dared to do this day for love. And if there's no one, I will know how to confront that accursed man myself for this murder, gliding in the midst of the women and servants who flatter the couple with their good wishes, aborting those precocious wishes by emptying this flask into the marriage cup!

Yacoub. Poison!

Beren. Poison. But don't come to me afterwards, you slave, talking of love and of regret. Do you still refuse? A quarter hour remains to me. That's more time than he'll need to die. Fifteen minutes—answer—will he die at your hand? Are you ready? Answer me, because I'm going in—talk!

Yacoub. Tomorrow—

Beren. Tomorrow! And this night, in that same room, he'll say
to her as he said to me, "I love you!" Tomorrow! And
what shall I do until then? Oh, you wish me to tear out
handfuls of my hair tonight, and split my forehead
against the walls, to become mad! Oh . . . tomorrow!
You're mocking me! And if this day is the last day and this
hellish night is going to last forever? God can order that
if it pleases Him! Tomorrow! And if I die of jealousy?
You're not jealous at all, you—not at all?

Yacoub. Oh!

Beren. If I told you: "In there, in his arms, the Count gave me
assurance of the most tender love . . . " Ah! You could
listen to me without wringing your hands, blaspheming,
feeling your hair stand on end and whiten at my voice.
Ah! you're not jealous. Listen, then . . .

Yacoub. Madam!

Beren. Listen. I loved him enough to deny my soul for him,
if he required it. Judge of my transports when he returned
after an absence! It was all cries, then; tears; ecstasy;
laughter; delirium lasting from night until day. . . . But
you don't understand. You're not jealous.

Yacoub. [*Taking out his dagger.*] Madam, kill me, for pity's sake,
or be silent!

Beren. Oh, it was joy that the angels could envy; the endless
exchange of words of love . . . All, in short, that the
soul and passion can invent . . .

Yacoub. And during that time, I . . . Oh, curses!

Beren. It was there, there! Are you looking? In that same
room!

Yacoub. Allah! You really want him.

Beren. I tell you I love him. That, in spite of this affront, a word of love from him could bring me back to his feet today. So—think about this—as long as he lives I'll escape you . . . Because I love him, do you understand?

Yacoub. When must I strike?

Beren. While he's living, the hope of returning still remains to me. With him dead, I'll love you with all of that other love. Isn't that right? Now do you feel he must die; die right now? If I waited an hour, do I know what my heart would want in an hour? Perhaps I would say to you, "Stop!"

Yacoub. I'm ready. Give your orders.

Beren. He must die in that room. Don't you see? His feet must trip over his grave as he walks to that bed—Because he's going to return to that room, leading his new wife.

Yacoub. [*Trembling.*] There he is!

[*The Count is seen advancing, leading his new wife. Two pages with torches precede him. Vassals and servants surround him, all crying.*] Long live our Countess!

Beren. By hell!

All. Long live the Count!

Beren. Do you think the vengeance will equal the shame? Do you hesitate?

Yacoub. No.

Beren. Hurry! Hurry! You only have an instant to go in before he does. See! But go, then! Oh, misery! What's stopping

you? What do I have to do in my turn? I'm ready . . .
Talk . . . Do you want to deceive me, Yacoub, in the
end? There won't be any time . . . Damnation! [*She
pushes him. He goes into the bedroom.*] At last!

[*She throws herself behind the prayer stool. With the
pages preceding him, the Count goes into the bedroom.
The pages put two torches down, and leave. During this
time the vassals cry.*] Long live the Count!

Count. [*Throwing a fistful of gold.*] For all of you!

All. Long live our countess!

Count. My lovely bride, come, give largesse, and all these
voices will pray to heaven for you.

[*The young bride throws her purse.*]

All. Long live the Count!

Count. Good, my children. Leave now.

[*They all leave by the door to the rear. The Count and his
wife go into the room. As the torches recede into the distance, the theatre returns to darkness, and Berengaria
stands up slowly.*]

Beren. [*Alone.*] Pray. He told you to. It will be for his soul; for
the angel of death is there to claim it. And if any of you,
by chance, cares for me, let him pray for mine also! [*Trembling.*] Did I hear . . . ? No; nothing. If his courage
failed! That could happen. Oh, rage! I should have used
this poison for him [*she takes the flask from her breast*] and
saved the dagger for me. Treason! What's he waiting
for?. . . . Well?

Count. [*Struck behind the scenes.*] Aah!

Beren. There he falls! [*She swallows the poison.*] Savoisy . . .
save a place in your tomb for me.

Young Countess. [*In the room.*] Help! Help!

Yacoub. [*Entering backwards, his dagger in his hand.*] Let's flee —
he's coming.

Count. [*Dragging himself along, and lifting the tapestry.*] It's you
who's killed me, Yacoub.

Beren. [*Leaning with her two hands on Yacoub's shoulders, since his
body hides her from the Count, and making him kneel so that
the Count can see her.*] It wasn't him! But I!

Count. Berengaria!

Young Countess. [*Crossing the courtyard.*] Help! [*She falls in a
faint.*]

Count. [*Dying.*] Ah! Ah!

Yacoub. Now, woman, make me forget all of this, because it's
really vile. Come, then. You promised me you'd come.
I'm waiting. You're mine forever . . .

Beren. [*Eyes on the Count.*] A few moments more. Then I'll belong entirely to you.

Yacoub. Oh! Look! They're running here in answer to her
cries. Take care; we won't be able to flee . . . there'll be
no more time . . . They're coming, Berengaria!

Beren. Still wait; wait . . .

Yacoub. Oh, come! come! Delay is death right now. The courtyard is full . . . Look . . . Come on, then! [*Berengaria*

falls to her knees.] What's she doing? Berengaria, is this how you keep your word? Berengaria, do you hear? . . . Come on!

Beren. [*Dying.*] Here I am . . . Take me.

[*She falls, her mouth on the Count's.*]

Yacoub. [*Taking her by the hair and lifting her head.*] Oh, curses! Her face is pale . . . Her heart . . . [*He puts his hand there.*] It's stopped beating . . . Her hand [*Taking the flask he finds in it.*] The flask is empty!

Young Countess. [*Getting to her feet again, surrounded by all the Count's house.*] Help! Oh, come, come. Over here!

Andrew. What, the Count dead . . . and the Countess, too!

Yacoub. Dead.

Andrew. Our master!

All. [*Leaning over him.*] Oh!

Yacoub. Good. You who were born on his land and wear the hereditary chain like dogs—stay howling by the open tomb. As for Yacoub . . . [*Taking the Count's parchment and showing it.*] He's free! He's returning to the desert!

ABOUT THE TRANSLATOR

DOROTHY TRENCH-BONETT is a Belizean of African descent. She grew up in the United States, however, and has been a citizen of this country since 1972. She is a graduate of Stuyvesant High School and of Yale University, where she received both her B.A. and M.A. She has also studied in Paris with a Sweetbrier Junior Year Abroad Program and in Taiwan at the Taipei Language Institute. Ms. Trench-Bonett has previously published short fiction and has written about the Afro-Russian poet Alexander Pushkin. She lives in Maryland with her husband and her two sons and is currently at work on a novel.

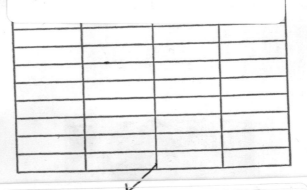